INTERNATIONAL ADOPTION

by
Margaret C. Jasper

Oceana's Legal Almanac Series:
Law for the Layperson

2003
Oceana Publications, Inc.
Dobbs Ferry, New York

You may order this or any Oceana publication by visiting Oceana's website at http://www.oceanalaw.com or contacting Customer Service at 1.914.693.8100 (domestic or international) or 1.800.831.0758 (U.S. only).

Library of Congress Control Number: 2003106568

ISBN: 0-379-11377-5

Oceana's Legal Almanac Series: Law for the Layperson
ISSN 1075-7376

©2003 by Oceana Publications, Inc.

Manufactured in the United States of America on acid-free paper.

To My Husband Chris

Your love and support
are my motivation and inspiration

-and-

In memory of my son, Jimmy

Table of Contents

CHAPTER 3:
OBTAINING AN IMMIGRANT VISA FOR THE ADOPTED CHILD

CHAPTER 4:
APPLYING FOR U.S. CITIZENSHIP FOR THE ADOPTED CHILD

CHAPTER 5:
THE INTERCOUNTRY ADOPTION ACT OF 2000

ABOUT THE AUTHOR

MARGARET C. JASPER is an attorney engaged in the general practice of law in South Salem, New York, concentrating in the areas of personal injury and entertainment law. Ms. Jasper holds a Juris Doctor degree from Pace University School of Law, White Plains, New York, is a member of the New York and Connecticut bars, and is certified to practice before the United States District Courts for the Southern and Eastern Districts of New York, the United States Court of Appeals for the Second Circuit, and the United States Supreme Court.

Ms. Jasper has been appointed to the panel of arbitrators of the American Arbitration Association and the law guardian panel for the Family Court of the State of New York, is a member of the Association of Trial Lawyers of America, and is a New York State licensed real estate broker and member of the Westchester County Board of Realtors, operating as Jasper Real Estate, in South Salem, New York. Margaret Jasper maintains a website at http://www.JasperLawOffice.com.

Ms. Jasper is the author and general editor of the following legal almanacs: AIDS Law; The Americans with Disabilities Act; Animal Rights Law; The Law of Attachment and Garnishment; Bankruptcy Law for the Individual Debtor; Individual Bankruptcy and Restructuring; Banks and their Customers; The Law of Buying and Selling; The Law of Capital Punishment; The Law of Child Custody; Commercial Law; Consumer Rights Law; The Law of Contracts; Copyright Law; Credit Cards and the Law; The Law of Debt Collection; Dictionary of Selected Legal Terms; The Law of Dispute Resolution; The Law of Drunk Driving; Education Law; Elder Law; Employee Rights in the Workplace; Employment Discrimination Under Title VII; Environmental Law; Estate Planning; Everyday Legal Forms; Harassment in the Workplace; Health Care and Your Rights. Home Mortgage Law Primer; Hospital Liability Law; Identity Theft and How To Protect Yourself; Insurance Law; The Law of Immigration; Juvenile Justice and Children's Law; Labor Law; Landlord-Tenant Law; The Law of Libel and Slander; Marriage and Divorce; The Law of Medical Malpractice; Motor Vehicle Law; The Law of No-Fault Insurance; The Law of Obscenity and Pornography; Patent Law; The Law of Personal Injury; Probate Law; The Law of Product Liability; Real Estate Law for the Homeowner and Broker; Religion and the Law; The Right to Die; Law for the Small Business Owner; Social Security Law; Special Education Law; The Law of Speech and the First Amendment; Trademark Law; Victim's Rights Law; The Law of Violence Against Women; Welfare: Your Rights and the Law; and Workers' Compensation Law.

INTRODUCTION

There are many citizens in the United States who have hopes of adopting a child. However, there are fewer and fewer children in America who are available for adoption. Therefore, many citizens have looked to countries outside of the United States for children who are in need of adoptive families. Thousands of children are brought to the United States each year by parents who have either adopted them abroad, or who seek to finalize, in America, an adoption of a child born abroad.

This almanac provides an overview of international adoption, and discusses the steps prospective adoptive parents must take to adopt a child from abroad, and obtain United States citizenship for that child. This almanac also discusses the applicable immigration laws which must be complied with in order to legally bring an adoptive, or prospective adoptive, child born abroad to the United States.

The proper processing of the child according to the Bureau of Citizenship and Immigration Services (BCIS) requirements is essential to avoid unnecessary delays. In particular, the BCIS requires a thorough investigation of the adoption case prior to permitting the child to emigrate to the United States. Prospective adoptive parents are advised to obtain reputable legal counsel experienced in international adoption to assist in the case.

Unfortunately, there are a number of disreputable agencies and individuals who prey upon prospective adoptive parents. This almanac provides information concerning some of the illegal and unscrupulous practices which a prospective adoptive parent may encounter in pursuing an international adoption.

The Appendix provides resource directories, applicable statutes, and other pertinent information and data. The Glossary contains definitions of many of the terms used throughout the almanac.

CHAPTER 1:
OVERVIEW OF INTERNATIONAL ADOPTION

IN GENERAL

The adoption of a child from abroad by an individual or couple is a private legal matter which is carried out under the laws and regulations of a foreign government. However, the process is not as easy as selecting a child and then simply bringing the child back to live with the adoptive parents in the United States. Procedures have been established which are designed to protect the child, the adoptive parent, and the birth parent.

Adoption procedures vary according to country. In general, most foreign countries require that the adoptive child is legally recognized as an orphan or, if there is a living parent, that the child is legally and irrevocably released for adoption by the parent. Most countries also require that the adoption proceeding be completed in the foreign court.

Certain countries require a period of residence by one or both adoptive parents. In these countries, prospective adoptive parents may find it necessary to spend an extended period of time in the foreign country awaiting the completion of the international adoption documents.

Some countries do allow for a "simple adoption," which means that the adoptive parent can be granted guardianship of the child by the foreign court. This allows the child to leave the foreign country so that the adoption proceedings can be completed in the country of the adoptive parents. A minority of countries allow adoptive parents to adopt through a third party without actually traveling to that country.

Nevertheless, it is important to note that a foreign country's determination that the child is an orphan does not guarantee that the child will be considered an orphan under governing United States law, The Immigration and Nationality Act (INA), since the foreign country may use different standards to make this determination.

In most cases, the formal adoption of a child in a foreign court is legally acceptable in the United States. However, a state court is not automatically required to recognize a foreign adoption decree and the status of the adopted child may be subject to challenge in a state court unless an adoption decree is entered in a state in the United States.

To prevent any challenges to the validity of the international adoption, it is recommended that a child adopted abroad be re-adopted in the court of the adoptive parent's state of residence as a precautionary measure. Once the child is re-adopted in the state court, the adoptive parents can request that a state birth certificate be issued, which will be recognized in all other states.

Under certain circumstances, the re-adoption of an adopted child born abroad is required under U.S. law. This is the case, for example, when the adoptive parent, or one of the adoptive parents if it is a married couple, did not see the child prior to or during the international adoption process. In that case, the child must be re-adopted in the United States even if a full final adoption decree has been issued in the foreign country.

It is crucial that all of these issues be considered prior to initiating the adoption process. Therefore, the prospective adoptive parent is advised to consult with an attorney who is fully familiar with both the laws of the foreign country where the child resides, and the requirements under United States law.

CHOOSING THE COUNTRY

It is important to carefully consider the foreign country from which one chooses to adopt a child. Some countries do not permit adoption and will grant legal custody only so long as the applicant for custody resides in that country. This is often the case in countries that apply Islamic law, and children from such countries do not qualify for immigrant status in the United States.

Many prospective adoptive parents are admirably concerned for the health and welfare of children who live in unstable countries where there exists social and political upheaval. However, adopting a child from a country embroiled in chaos may be extremely difficult to complete. For example, it may be difficult to locate documents necessary to fulfill the legal requirements for adoption and immigration to the United States.

In addition, when a parent is missing, it is often difficult to determine whether the child is truly an orphan or whether the child has been temporarily abandoned or involuntarily separated from a parent caught up in a hostile situation. Further, there is a greater chance that the prospective adoptive parent will be taken advantage of by unscrupulous parties who may provide false documentation or otherwise try to process an illegal adoption for financial gain.

These problems can lead to lengthy delays and emotional anguish if the adoption process falls through and/or the adopted child is not permitted to enter the United States. Thus, when considering the adoption of a child from a country in social or political crisis, the prospective adoptive parent is strongly cautioned to contact the U.S. Department of State (DOS) and the U.S. Bureau of Citizenship and Immigration Services (BCIS), an agency organized under the newly-formed Department of Homeland Security, for further information concerning the particular country before going forward with the adoption process.

ELIGIBILITY TO ADOPT A CHILD FROM ABROAD

As previously stated, the adoption of a child from abroad by an individual or couple is a private legal matter which is carried out under the laws and regulations of a foreign government. However, it is important to note that simply adopting a child born abroad in a foreign country does not guarantee that the adopted child will gain entry into the United States.

As set forth below, following an international adoption, only a U.S. citizen may file a petition with the BCIS for the immediate immigration of the adopted child to the United States. There is no way an orphan can legally immigrate to the United States without being processed through, and approved by the BCIS.

International Adoption by a United States Citizen

Under the INA, an unmarried U.S. citizen who is at least twenty-five years of age, or a married U.S. citizen and his or her spouse, of any age, may file a petition for the immigration of an adopted child to the United States. The spouse of a married citizen does not have to be a citizen, but must be legally in this country and also agree to the adoption.

The Two-Year Co-Residency Provision

The INA provides immigrant classification for "a child adopted while under the age of sixteen years if the child has been in the legal custody of, and has resided with, the adoptive parent for at least two years."

This provision is generally referred to as the "two-year provision," and usually pertains to U.S. citizens who are temporarily residing abroad and wish to adopt a child in accordance with the laws of the foreign country where they reside. In such cases, the two-year co-residency requirement will be satisfied while the adoptive parent and child reside abroad.

The Orphan Petition

Most adoptive parents, however, are not able to spend two years living abroad with the child. Thus, they must acquire immigrant classification for the child under Section 101(b)(1)(F) of the INA, which grants immigrant classification to orphans who have been adopted, or will be adopted by United States citizens. The process is initiated by filing a petition, generally referred to as an "orphan petition," with the BCIS. The orphan petition process is discussed in detail in Chapter 2 of this almanac.

Under this provision, both the child and the adoptive parents must satisfy a number of requirements established by the INA and the related regulations, but the two-year residency requirement is eliminated. If the orphan petition is approved, the child is considered to be an immediate relative of a United States citizen, and the child can obtain an immigrant visa immediately without being placed on a visa waiting list. Nevertheless, the child must still qualify for an immigrant visa just like any other person born abroad. The immigrant visa application process is discussed in more detail in Chapter 3 of this almanac.

When the adopted child enters the United States with the immigrant visa, the child is considered to be a lawful permanent resident of the United States, not a U.S. citizen. However, due to recent changes in immigration law, in some situations, a child will automatically become a United States citizen immediately upon admission into the United States as a lawful permanent resident.

The acquisition of U.S. citizenship for an adopted child born abroad is discussed in more detail in Chapter 4 of this almanac.

Orphan Status

Under the INA, a child born abroad is defined as an orphan if the child does not have any parents because of the death or disappearance of, abandonment or desertion by, or separation or loss from, both parents. A child born abroad is also an orphan if his or her sole or surviving parent is not able to take proper care of the child and has, in writing, irrevocably released the child for emigration and adoption.

In order for the child to gain entry to the United States, the orphan petition must be filed before the child's 16th birthday. An exception exists allowing the petition to be filed before the child's 18th birthday if the child is a natural sibling of another orphan or adopted child, and is adopted with or following that child by the same adoptive parents.

International Adoption by a Non-U.S. Citizen

A person who is not a United States citizen, such as a legal permanent resident or long-term non-immigrant visa holder, may not file a petition for the entry of an adopted child born abroad to the United States, and will not be able to bring an adopted child who is born abroad to the United States. Thus, a non-citizen is strongly advised not to adopt a child born abroad unless and until they are able to obtain United States citizenship themselves.

Under the INA, a legal permanent resident or long-term nonimmigrant visa holder is permitted to bring their spouse and children with them upon entry to the United States, or provide for their immigration at a later date. The definition of "child" under this provision includes: (1) biological children; (2) step-children; and (3) adopted children.

However, because the INA defines an "adopted child" as one who has been adopted before the age of sixteen, and who has resided with, and been in the legal custody of, the parent for two years, this two-year co-residency provision acts as a bar to the non-citizen in adopting a child born abroad.

Thus, whereas a child born abroad to a non-citizen after the non-citizen enters the United States, is eligible to receive a dependent visa, a child who is adopted in a foreign country must first meet the two-year co-residency requirement before being eligible to emigrate to the United States. Insofar as the INA does not permit a non-citizen to bring the adopted child born abroad into the United States to fulfill the two-year co-residency requirement, it is impossible for the child to obtain a dependent visa under the Act.

Long-Term Nonimmigrant Visa Holders

In the case of a nonimmigrant visa holder, in order to have an internationally-adopted child join them in the United States, the visa holder must leave the United States and live abroad with the adopted child for two years to fulfill the co-residency requirement. The visa holder can then receive a dependent visa for the adopted child for future visits to the United States.

Long term nonimmigrant visa classes include: E1/E2 Treaty Traders or Investors, F-1 Students, I Journalists, J-1 Exchange Visitors, H, O, or P Visa Temporary Workers, L-1 Intra-company Transfers, and R-1 Religious Workers. Different rules cover diplomats and officials in the

United States on A or G visas, and the U.S. Department of State, or embassy or international organization employing the individual should be contacted for further information.

Legal Permanent Residents

In the case of a legal permanent resident, the provisions of the INA produce a more difficult scenario because a legal permanent resident is not permitted to reside outside of the United States. This provision makes it impossible for the legal permanent resident to fulfill the two-year co-residency requirement in order to petition for the adopted child's entry into the United States.

Nevertheless, once a legal permanent resident naturalizes as a United States citizen, he or she may petition for the immediate immigration of an adopted, or prospective adopted, child born abroad to the United States.

ROLE OF THE U.S. GOVERNMENT IN INTERNATIONAL ADOPTION

Although a number of agencies of the United States government provide information to prospective adoptive parents on the various aspects of the international adoption process, United States authorities do not get involved on the parent's behalf with the courts in the country where the adoption is supposed to take place.

The U.S. Department of State

As set forth below, the U.S. Department of State (DOS) provides detailed information on the adoption process in various foreign countries. Because international adoption is a private matter between the prospective adoptive parents and a sovereign foreign country, the DOS cannot intervene in the foreign courts on behalf of the parents, however, the DOS does provide the following information and services:

1. The DOS can provide information about international adoption in over 60 foreign countries;

2. The DOS can provide information about U.S. visa requirements for international adoption;

3. The DOS can make inquiries of the U.S. consular section abroad regarding the status of a specific adoption case, and clarify documentation or other requirements; and

4. The DOS can ensure that U.S. citizens are not discriminated against by foreign authorities or courts.

The DOS cannot undertake any of the following actions:

1. The DOS cannot locate a child available for adoption;

2. The DOS cannot become directly involved in the adoption process in another country;

3. The DOS cannot act as an attorney or represent adoptive parents in court; and

4. The DOS cannot order that an adoption take place or that a visa be issued.

The Office of Children's Issues, a division of the Department of State's Bureau of Consular Affairs, formulates, develops and coordinates policies and programs and provides direction to foreign service posts on international adoption.

Adoption information is made available on a 24 hour basis through the DOS website (http://travel.state.gov/); via recorded telephone information at (202) 736-7000; and through an automated facsimile system at (202) 312-9743. Written requests for information on international adoption may be sent to the DOS at the following address:

Office of Children's Issues
U.S. Department of State
CA/OCS/CI
1800 G Street, NW, Suite 2100
Washington, D.C. 20006

CHAPTER 2:
PROCESSING THE
INTERNATIONAL ADOPTION

IN GENERAL

In order to complete an international adoption and bring to the United States an adopted child born abroad, the prospective adoptive parents must fulfill all of the requirements established by the United States Bureau of Citizenship and Immigration Services (BCIS), as well as the laws and regulations of the foreign country in which the child resides. There may be additional requirements established by the state of residence of the adoptive parent.

APPLICATION FOR ADVANCE PROCESSING OF AN ORPHAN PETITION

The prospective adoptive parent may apply for advanced processing of a child even before they actually find a child to adopt. Although this is not required, doing so may make the adoption process faster once a child is chosen for adoption. In fact, it is generally advisable for all prospective adoptive parents to apply for advance processing to ensure that the BCIS expeditiously makes the determination that relates to their ability to provide a proper home environment, and their suitability as a parent, before they adopt a child in a foreign country.

The Application for Advance Processing of an Orphan Petition (Form I-600A) is filed with the BCIS. A prospective petitioner residing in the United States should file the petition with the BCIS office which has jurisdiction over the petitioner's place of residence. A prospective petitioner residing outside the United States should consult the nearest U.S. Consulate or Embassy.

As stated above, in processing the application, the BCIS determines whether a prospective adoptive parent will be able to properly care for an orphan. As further discussed below, the BCIS relies on a thorough home study report and FBI fingerprint clearances in making their determination.

The application for advance processing may be filed by anyone eligible to file an orphan petition, as discussed in Chapter 1 of this almanac. In addition, an unmarried U.S. citizen may file an application for advance processing if they are at least 24 years of age and will be at least 25 when the child is adopted and an orphan petition is filed on the child's behalf with the BCIS.

A sample Application for Advance Processing of an Orphan Petition (Form I-600A) is set forth at Appendix 1.

An approved I-600A Application is valid for eighteen (18) months. During those eighteen months, a Petition to Classify the Orphan as an Immediate Relative must be filed, as set forth below.

The prospective adoptive parent may request that a duplicate approval notice be sent to the U.S. Consulate or Embassy in another country. This may expedite processing if the prospective adoptive parent should choose to adopt a child living in a country other than the one originally intended.

A sample Application for Action on an Approved Application or Petition (Form I-824) is set forth at Appendix 2.

PETITION TO CLASSIFY ORPHAN AS IMMEDIATE RELATIVE

In all instances, the adoptive, or prospective adoptive, parent is required to file a Petition to Classify the Orphan as an Immediate Relative (Form I-600). The purpose of the petition is to classify an orphan born abroad who either is, or will be, adopted by a U.S. citizen as an immediate relative of the U.S. citizen in order to allow the child to enter the United States. The petition is filed by the U.S. citizen who is adopting the child, along with the required fee.

A petitioner residing in the United States should file the petition with the BCIS office which has jurisdiction over the petitioner's place of residence. A petitioner residing outside the United States should consult the nearest U.S. Consulate or Embassy.

If the adoptive parents have already submitted an I-600A advance processing application to the BCIS, and an approval notice has been forwarded to the U.S. Consulate or Embassy in the child's home country, the adoptive parent may file the I-600 petition in person at that Consulate or Embassy.

If there is no BCIS office in the country of adoption, a consular officer is authorized to approve the I-600 petition, relying upon the approved I-600A advance processing application as demonstration of the suitability of the adoptive parent, and their compliance with any applicable state pre-adoption requirements.

Only one adoptive parent must be physically present to file the I-600 petition overseas, however, that parent must be a U.S. citizen. A third party may not file the petition on the parents' behalf, even with a valid Power of Attorney. In addition, if only one of the two adoptive parents travels to the foreign country, the petition must nevertheless be properly signed by both parents after it has been completely filled out. This means one parent cannot sign for the other parent, and neither parent may sign the petition until all the details about the child have been entered on the form.

A sample Petition to Classify an Orphan as an Immediate Relative (Form I-600) is set forth at Appendix 3.

If an I-600A advance processing application has not already been filed in the case, then the petitioner will also be required to submit the documentation that would normally have been submitted with the I-600A application at the time the I-600 petition is filed, as set forth below.

REQUIRED DOCUMENTATION

The international adoption procedure involves the production of numerous documents. In general, the adoption agency, adoption attorney, foreign court, U.S. Embassy, BCIS, and the adoptive parent's state of residence may require some or all of the following items:

1. Birth Certificate for the Adoptive Parent;

2. Child Abuse Clearance for the Adoptive Parent;

3. Divorce/Death Certificate;

4. Financial Statement of the Adoptive Parent;

5. Foreign Adoption/Custody Decree;

6. Foreign Birth Certificate for the Child;

7. Foreign Passport for the Child;

8. Home Study Report;

9. Letters of Recommendation;

10. Orphan Status Document;

11. Photographs of the Family;

12. Photographs of the Child;

13. Physician's Report for the Adoptive Parent;

14. Physician's Report for the Child;

15. Police Certificate;

16. Power of Attorney;

17. Verification of Employment of the Adoptive Parent; and

18. An IRS 1040 Tax Return for the Adoptive Parent.

There may be additional documents which the adoptive parent may be required to produce by various private and government agencies in connection with the international adoption.

Authentication of Documents

Some countries require that the required documentation be authenticated. For example, birth, death and marriage certificates must bear the seal of the government office issuing the record, and be authenticated by the U.S. Department of State Authentication Office. There is a fee per document for the authentication service. Further information may be obtained by contacting:

The U.S. Department of State Authentication Office
518 23rd Street, N.W.
Washington, DC 20520
Telephone: 202-647-5002

FINGERPRINT REQUIREMENTS

The law requires that all prospective adoptive parents, and all adults age 18 and over who are members of the prospective adoptive parent's household, provide fingerprints to the BCIS for completion of FBI background checks. After receiving an I-600 petition, or an I-600A advance processing application, the BCIS will send appointment letters with the date and location for all prospective adoptive parents and adult members of the household to appear for fingerprinting. The persons to be fingerprinted must bring the appointment letters to the BCIS fingerprint location on the appointment date. There is a fee for each person who is required to undergo a fingerprint check.

If the prospective adoptive parent and any adult member of the household lives abroad, they are also required to be fingerprinted, however, they are exempt from the fingerprint fee. The prospective adoptive parent and any adult member of the household residing abroad must have their fingerprint cards prepared by the BCIS, or by a United States consular officer at a United States Embassy or Consulate abroad, or at a

United States military installation abroad. U.S. State Department consular officers and U.S. military offices are authorized to charge a fee for this service. The completed fingerprint cards must be submitted with the I-600 petition or I-600A advance processing application.

The FBI background check is one of the primary tools used by the BCIS to determine the ability of prospective adoptive parents to provide a proper home environment for an orphan, and their suitability as parents.

The FBI fingerprint checks are valid for fifteen (15) months. The I-600 petition may not be approved without current FBI fingerprint records for the prospective adoptive parent and all adult members of the prospective adoptive parent's household. Thus, it may be necessary to provide fingerprints more than once in order to comply with immigration regulations.

When more than one petition is submitted by the same petitioner for orphans who are also siblings, only one set of petition and fingerprinting fees is required. However, when more than one petition is submitted for orphans who are not siblings, both the filing fee and fingerprint fees must be submitted for each petition.

THE HOME STUDY REPORT

A home study report, which is prepared by a licensed social worker or other authorized person, is required by both the foreign government and the BCIS in connection with the petition. Some countries will accept a properly authenticated home study report, whereas other countries will require a personal appearance by the adoptive parent before the foreign court. Several countries also require a post-adoption follow-up report which is generally conducted by the adoption agency or the foreign country's consul in the United States.

The Home Study Preparer

The home study report is administered by a home study preparer. The home study preparer conducts the research and preparation for the home study report, including the required personal interviews. The home study preparer must be an individual or organization licensed or otherwise authorized to conduct the research and preparation for a home study under the laws of the state of the adopted child's proposed residence, and may include a public agency with authority under the state's law in adoption matters, and a public or private adoption agency licensed or otherwise authorized under the state's law to place children for adoption.

If the adoptive parents reside abroad, and the child's adoption has been finalized abroad, the home study preparer may include any party licensed or otherwise authorized to conduct home studies under the law of any state of the United States, or any party licensed or otherwise authorized by the foreign country's adoption authorities to conduct home studies under the laws of the foreign country.

Timing of the Home Study

The home study report must be submitted within one year of the filing date of the I-600A advanced processing application, and the report, or a recent update of the report, must not be more than six months old at the time it is submitted to the BCIS.

If a home study update is submitted, a copy of the original home study report must accompany the update. Once submitted, the report will not have to be updated unless there is some significant change prior to the adopted child's immigration into the United States. Examples of changes which would be considered significant and would require an update include but are not limited to changes in the adopted parent's residence; marital status; criminal history; financial resources; and the addition of one or more children or other dependents to the adopted family.

Scope of the Home Study Evaluation

Personal Interviews and Home Visits

In conducting the home study, the home study preparer is required to schedule at least one home visit, and at least one interview, in person, with the prospective adoptive parents and any adult member of the prospective adoptive parent's household.

Assessment of Ability to Parent

In determining the prospective adoptive parent's ability to properly parent the adopted child, the home study preparer will evaluate the physical, mental and emotional health of the prospective adoptive parent, and assess any potential problem areas. Based on this assessment, and any outside evaluations that have been conducted, the home study report should include any recommended restrictions on the characteristics of the prospective adopted child.

If any issues arise during the evaluation that are beyond the scope of the home study preparer's expertise, a referral must be made to an appropriate licensed professional for further evaluation.

Financial Assessment

The home study preparer must make an assessment of the financial resources available to support the prospective adopted child without considering income designated for the support of the prospective adopted parent's other children or household members. The prospective adoptive parent's financial situation, including a description of their income, financial resources, debts, and expenses, must be included, along with a statement of the evidence reviewed to verify the financial situation, e.g. tax returns, income statements, etc.

Background of Criminal Behavior or Abuse

The home study preparer must also examine each prospective adoptive parent, and adult member of the household, concerning whether he or she has had a history or allegations of any type of criminal behavior; substance abuse; sexual or child abuse; or domestic violence, even if the act did not result in an arrest or conviction.

The home study preparer is also required to check the records of any available child abuse registry for each of the prospective adoptive parents, and for each adult member of the prospective adoptive parent's household, to determine whether any such allegations have been made or reports filed.

If it is determined that there is a history of criminal behavior or abuse, the home study report must contain an evaluation of the suitability of the prospective adoptive home, including information concerning all arrests or convictions; details of any disclosed substance abuse, sexual or child abuse, and/or domestic violence, and the date of each such occurrence.

The home study preparer should also include in the report, a certified copy of any documentation showing final disposition of any incident which resulted in arrest, indictment, conviction, and/or any judicial judgement or administrative action, as well as a signed statement from the prospective adoptive parent detailing any such incident.

If it has been determined that a prospective adoptive parent or an adult member of the household has a criminal history, or a history of substance abuse, sexual or child abuse, and/or domestic violence, and the home study preparer nevertheless makes a decision in favor of the adoption, the home study report must also include an evaluation of the seriousness of the incident, a thorough discussion of the rehabilitation efforts which demonstrates that the prospective adoptive parent is and will be able to provide proper care for the orphan, and the home study preparer's detailed reasons for making a favorable recommendation.

If the prospective adoptive parent or any adult member of the household fails to disclose information relating to any of the above, this failure may result in the denial of the advanced processing application and petition.

Prior Home Study Reports

If the prospective adoptive parent has previously received an unfavorable home study report and/or has previously been rejected for adoption, the current home study report should include a copy of each such previous report and the findings and reasons for the prior negative determination.

Living Accommodations

The home study must include a detailed description and assessment of the current living accommodations of the prospective adoptive home, and the prospective accommodations if there are plans for relocating. If the prospective adoptive parent resides abroad, a description of the future living accommodations in the United States must be included, if known.

Approval and Certification

If the home study preparer makes a favorable recommendation, the report must include the preparer's specific approval and a discussion of their findings and reasons for approval; the number of children that may be adopted by the prospective adoptive parent; and any restrictions concerning the prospective adoptive child, such as nationality, age or gender.

The home study preparer must also certify that they are licensed or otherwise authorized to conduct the home study.

Review of the Home Study Report

If the prospective adoptive parents reside in a state which requires the state to review the home study, such review must take place before the home study is submitted. If the prospective adoptive parent resides abroad, an appropriately licensed or authorized public or private adoption agency must review the home study before it is submitted.

APPELLATE REVIEW

If a prospective adoptive parent's petition is denied, they will be sent a denial letter which provides details on how to appeal the decision. Generally, a Notice of Appeal must be filed with the office that issued the denial letter within 33 days of receiving the denial. A fee must also accompany the Notice of Appeal. The appeal is then referred to the Administrative Appeals Unit in Washington, D.C.

A sample Notice of Appeal to the Administrative Appeals Unit (AAU) (Form I-290B) is set forth at Appendix 4.

CHAPTER 3:
OBTAINING AN IMMIGRANT VISA FOR THE ADOPTED CHILD

THE VISA APPLICATION

When the international adoption or guardianship proceeding is completed, the adoptive parent must apply for an immigrant visa for the child. An orphan cannot be brought to the United States without a visa, which is based upon the approval of a petition filed with the U.S. Bureau of Citizenship and Immigration Services (BCIS), as discussed in Chapter 2.

A table containing the number of immigrant visas issued to orphans coming to the United States from 1989 through 2002 is set forth at Appendix 5.

Tables containing the number of immigrant visas issued to orphans coming to the United States, by top twenty countries of origin, for fiscal years 2001 and 2002 are set forth at Appendix 6 and Appendix 7, respectively.

The type of visa varies depending on whether the child was adopted abroad or whether the child is to be adopted in the United States. The application is made to the U.S. Consular office of the country where the child resides, which will schedule a visa interview and visual inspection of the child prior to issuing the visa. It should be noted, however, that the issuance of a visa does not automatically ensure entry to the United States. The child must still be approved by the BCIS.

Thus, it is prudent for the adoptive parents to meet with the U.S. Consulate officer early in the process to discuss any questions or concerns they may have about the prospective adoption, and to obtain a list of visa requirements, including necessary forms and documentation.

At the final visa interview, the consular office will: (1) review the I-600 petition; (2) verify the identity of the child and the child's status as an orphan as defined by the Immigration and Nationality Act (INA); (3) ensure that the adoptive parents have legal custody; (4) review the child's medical report; and (5) make sure the child has the necessary travel documentation.

DOCUMENTATION

Documentation required in connection with a visa application generally includes:

1. Notification by the BCIS of approval of the I-600A application for advanced processing or I-600 petition;

2. The final adoption decree or proof of custody from the foreign government;

3. The child's birth certificate;

4. The child's passport from the country of the child's nationality;

5. The completed and signed medical examination report;

6. Necessary photographs of the child;

7. The visa application (Form OF 230)

8. A completed I-600 petition if the BCIS approval was based on an I-600A application, and an I-600 petition was not previously filed with or approved by the BCIS.

ORPHAN INVESTIGATION

When an adoptive, or prospective adoptive parent, applies with the U.S. Consulate or Embassy for an immigrant visa for the child, an orphan investigation takes place as part of normal processing of the application. This investigation is conducted by a Department of State consular officer or an INS officer for those areas where INS has an office.

The purpose of the orphan investigation is to confirm that: (1) the child is an orphan as defined in U.S. immigration law; and (2) the child does not have an illness or disability that is not described in the I-600 petition.

Orphan Status

In processing the I-600 petition, the BCIS determines, among other things, whether the adopted, or prospective adopted, child meets the BCIS definition of an "orphan" so that the child can qualify for entry into the United States. Such a determination must be made in order for the I-600 petition to be approved.

When the visa application is filed, the U.S. Consulate or Embassy also makes a determination as to the status of the child as an orphan. If there are doubts about a particular child's eligibility as an orphan, the consular officer cannot approve the petition and must forward the case to BCIS.

If it is determined that the child is not, in fact, eligible for classification as an orphan under the U.S. immigration law, a notice of intent to revoke the approval of the I-600 petition will be issued. The petitioner is then permitted to submit evidence to overcome the stated grounds for revoking the approval.

The Medical Examination

Prior to issuance of a visa, a medical examination of the child must be performed by a physician who is approved by the U .S. Consulate or Embassy. The purpose of the medical examination is to make sure the child does not have any medical conditions which would cause him or her to be ineligible for a visa until treated.

The adoptive parent is advised to have a private medical examination of the child undertaken prior to the examination by the designated physician so that they are fully aware of the child's medical condition and can decide whether to delay the visa application.

If it is determined that the child has an illness or disability which has not been described in the I-600 petition, the adoptive parent is provided with details about the medical condition. The adoptive parent may then decide whether they still want to bring the child to the United States as an immigrant. If the adoptive parent decides to bring such a child to the United States, they should be advised that the child must still be admissible to the United States.

Some illnesses will make a child inadmissible to the United States. For example, if the child has a communicable disease of public health significance, that child may be inadmissible. Most of these grounds of inadmissibility may be waived if certain conditions are met, and the adoptive parent will be advised of the requirements that must be met before the child may legally enter the United States.

Processing Time

The orphan investigation can be a time-consuming process. The officer will make every effort to expedite the investigation; however, the process can still be lengthy. Before making travel arrangements, the adoptive parent going abroad for processing should contact the appropriate

American Embassy or Consulate, or BCIS overseas office, for details on processing times.

VACCINATIONS EXEMPTION

Section 212(a)(1)(A)(ii) of the Immigration and Nationality Act requires that any person who seeks admission as an immigrant, or adjustment of status to the status of an alien lawfully admitted for permanent residence, shall present documentation of having received vaccinations against diseases that are preventable by vaccination, such as mumps, measles, rubella, polio, tetanus and diphtheria toxoids, pertussis, influenze type B, hepatitis B, varicella and pneumoccocal.

This section exempts from the immunization requirement a child who is: (1) 10 years of age or younger; (2) described in Section 101(b)(1)(F); and (3) seeking an immigrant visa as an immediate relative under section 201(b), provided that the adoptive parent or prospective adoptive parent, prior to the child's admission, executes an affidavit stating that the parent is aware of the provisions of subparagraph (A)(ii) and will ensure that, within 30 days of the child's admission, or at the earliest time that is medically appropriate, the child will receive the vaccinations identified in such subparagraph.

A sample Affidavit Concerning Exemption from Immigrant Vaccination Requirements for a Foreign Adopted Child (Form DS1981) is set forth at Appendix 8.

TYPE OF IMMIGRANT VISA

The law distinguishes between orphans who are adopted in the foreign country, and orphans coming to the United States for adoption. An orphan who has been fully adopted in the foreign country may receive an IR-3 visa. To qualify for an IR-3 visa, the child must have been seen by both parents prior to or during the adoption proceedings.

An orphan who has not been fully adopted in the foreign country, e.g., where the parents are given guardianship of the child by the foreign court, or a child who was not seen by the adoptive parents prior to the adoption's finalization, may obtain an IR-4 visa. Any child who enters the United States on an IR-4 immigrant visa must be re-adopted after the child enters the United States, in accordance with applicable laws of the state in which the family resides.

Therefore, before an IR-4 visa can be issued to the child, the U.S. Consulate officer must ensure that the pre-adoption requirements of the child's future state of residence have been met. Thus, the adoptive parents should determine in advance the requirements of their own particular state of residence.

CHAPTER 4:
APPLYING FOR U.S. CITIZENSHIP FOR THE ADOPTED CHILD

IN GENERAL

Prior to the enactment of the Child Citizenship Act of 2000, in order for an internationally-adopted child of an American citizen to acquire United States citizenship, the adoptive parent had to apply for citizenship on behalf of the child, and the child had to complete the naturalization process, and take the oath of allegiance. The child did not acquire citizenship until the Immigration and Naturalization Service (INS) approved the application. Occasionally, delays in this process resulted in an adopted child being subject to deportation from the United States.

However, under the Act, changes were made to Section 320 of the Immigration and Naturalization Act which permits certain eligible children born abroad to acquire citizenship automatically provided certain requirements are met. Thus, adopted children of United States citizens are now permanently protected from deportation.

Children who do not meet the requirements set forth in the Act must still acquire U.S. citizenship through the application and naturalization process. The automatic citizenship eligibility requirements under the Act, as well as the citizenship application and naturalization process, are further discussed below.

THE CHILD CITIZENSHIP ACT OF 2000

The Child Citizenship Act of 2000 was signed into law in October 2000, and became effective on February 27, 2001. Under the Act, certain adopted children born abroad, who currently reside permanently in the United States, can acquire United States citizenship automatically.

The text of The Child Citizenship Act of 2000 (Public Law 106-395) is set forth at Appendix 9.

In order to qualify for automatic citizenship under the Act, the following requirements must be met:

1. At least one parent of the child must be a U.S. citizen, either by birth or naturalization;

2. The child must be under the age of 18;

3. The child must currently be residing permanently in the United States in the legal and physical custody of the United States citizen parent;

4. The child must be a lawful permanent resident;

5. The child must meet the requirements applicable to adopted children under immigration law; and

6. The adoption must be final.

Under the Act, the internationally-adopted, as well as biological, child of an American citizen automatically acquires U.S. citizenship on the date they immigrate to the United States without having to apply for citizenship. The child's citizenship status is no longer dependent on an INS-approved naturalization application.

Adopted children who were already in the United States, were under the age of 18, and met all of the requirements under the Act, automatically acquired citizenship as of February 27, 2001, the date the Act became effective.

A child who does not meet all of those requirements acquires citizenship automatically on the date the child meets the necessary requirements. For example, A child who enters the United States on an IR-4 visa in anticipation of being adopted in the United States will automatically acquire American citizenship when the adoption is full and final in the United States. The child does not have to meet the requirements in any particular order.

Lawful Permanent Residence Status

Under the Act, it must be shown that the child is a lawful permanent resident of the United States. A child who has lawful permanent residence status will have a permanent resident card, commonly referred to as a "green card." Another way to demonstrate lawful permanent resident status is the I-551 stamp on the child's passport. This stamp shows that the child entered the United States on an immigrant visa and/or has been admitted as a lawful permanent resident.

Proof of Citizenship

Proof of citizenship, such as a citizenship certificate or passport, are not automatically issued to children who acquire citizenship under the Act. However, if proof of citizenship is sought, parents of eligible children may apply for a certificate of citizenship from the United States Bureau of Citizenship and Immigration Services (BCIS), or passport for their child from the U.S. Department of State (DOS).

Certificate of Citizenship

In order to apply for a Certificate of Citizenship for the adopted child who acquires automatic citizenship under the Act, certain documents must be submitted.

1. An Application for Certificate of Citizenship in Behalf of an Adopted Child (Form N-643);

2. The application fee;

3. Photographs of the child; and

4. An Application for Acquisition of Citizenship Through a Grandparent (Form N-643-Supplement A), if the child currently lives outside the United States, as further discussed below.

A sample Application for Certificate of Citizenship in Behalf of an Adopted Child (Form N-643) is set forth at Appendix 10.

For adopted children who immigrate to the United States, the adoptive parent is not required to submit any additional evidence that is already contained in the BCIS file.

If the child has not immigrated to the United States and does not have a "green card," in addition to the above required documents, the adoptive parent should also submit:

1. The child's birth certificate;

2. The adoptive parent's birth certificate;

3. The adoptive parent's marriage certificate, if applicable;

4. Evidence of termination of previous marriages, if applicable;

5. Evidence of the full and final adoption, if applicable;

6. Evidence of all legal name changes, if applicable.

If the adopted child lives in the United States, the application and supporting documents must be filed at the BCIS district office in the United States with jurisdiction over the adoptive parent's place of residence. If the adopted child lives abroad, the application and supporting documents may be filed at any BCIS district office in the United States. The adoptive parent and adopted child must travel to the United States to complete the application process.

Application for Acquisition of Citizenship Through a Grandparent

Under the Act, the U.S. citizen parent of a child living abroad must have five years of physical presence in the United States, or its outlying possessions, with at least two years occurring after age 14, in order to apply for citizenship on behalf of the child. If the citizen parent cannot meet this requirement, the law allows them to rely on the physical presence of the U.S. citizen grandparent to apply for citizenship. Under the Act, the U.S. citizen grandparent must be living in order to use that grandparent's residence to qualify the child for U.S. citizenship.

A sample Application for Acquisition of Citizenship Through a Grandparent (Form N-643-Supplement A) is set forth at Appendix 11.

United States Passport

In order to apply for a United States passport for the adoptive child who acquires automatic citizenship under the Act, the following documents must be submitted:

1. Proof of the child's relationship to the U.S. citizen parent. For an adopted child, this would be a certified copy of the final adoption decree, which must be translated if it is not in English;

2. The child's foreign passport showing the BCIS I-551 stamp in the passport, or the child's permanent resident card (green card);

3. Proof of identity of the U.S. citizen parent;

4. The passport application;

5. Passport photographs; and

6. The application filing fee.

CHILDREN AGE 18 AND OVER

The law was not enacted retroactively. Therefore, insofar as the law requires that a child be under the age of 18 in order for the automatic citizenship provision to apply, children who were age 18 or over on February 27, 2001 did not qualify for automatic citizenship even if they met all other criteria under the Act.

Adopted children age 18 and over who are not eligible under the Act must apply for naturalization and meet all of the eligibility requirements that currently exist for adult lawful permanent residents under the immigration law.

ADOPTED CHILDREN BORN ABROAD RESIDING OUTSIDE THE UNITED STATES

Under the Act, an adopted child born abroad who resides outside of the United States does not acquire automatic citizenship. In order for such a child to acquire U.S. citizenship, the adoptive parent must apply for naturalization on behalf of the child. This can be accomplished even if they do not have a permanent address in the United States. However, the naturalization process cannot take place overseas. The child must be in the United States, at least temporarily, to complete the naturalization process and take the oath of allegiance.

To be eligible for naturalization, a child must meet the definition of "child" for naturalization purposes under immigration law, and must also meet the following requirements:

1. The child must have at least one U.S. citizen parent, either by birth or naturalization;

2. The U.S. citizen parent must have been physically present in the United States for at least five years, at least two of which were after the age of 14, or the U.S. citizen parent must have a citizen parent who has been physically present in the United States for at least five years, at least two of which were after the age of 14;

3. The child must be under 18 years of age;

4. The child who is residing outside the United States in the legal and physical custody of the United States citizen parent, must have been lawfully admitted into the United States as a nonimmigrant.;

5. The child must be temporarily present in the United States, having entered the United States lawfully and maintaining lawful status in the United States;

6. The child must meet the requirements applicable to adopted children under immigration law;

7. If the naturalization application is approved, the child must take the same oath of allegiance administered to adult naturalization applicants. If the child is too young to understand the oath, the oath requirement may be waived.

The adoptive parent must obtain a B-2 visa for the child to enter the United States. To obtain the B-2 visa, the adoptive parent must demonstrate that the child qualifies either under the two-year custody rule, as previously discussed, or present an approved Form I-600 petition. When applying for a nonimmigrant visa, the adoptive parents must also prove that they have made all the necessary arrangements with the BCIS office and that they intend to depart the U.S. to continue their residence abroad. Naturalization in all cases must be completed before the child turns 18.

CHAPTER 5:
THE INTERCOUNTRY ADOPTION
ACT OF 2000

IN GENERAL

On October 6, 2000, the United States enacted the Intercountry Adoption Act of 2000 (IAA) in order to approve the provisions of the Hague Convention on Protection of Children and Cooperation in Respect of Intercountry Adoption (Hague Convention).

Implementation of the IAA will occur only after the Immigration and Naturalization Service (INS) and the U.S. Department of State (DOS) publish implementing regulations in the Federal Register, and the United States deposits the instruments of ratification with the Permanent Bureau of the Hague Conference.

Implementing regulations are expected to be published by October 2003. In the meantime, the adoption procedures under Section 101(b)(1)(E) and (F) of the INA will continue to govern all intercountry adoptions.

OBJECTIVES OF THE HAGUE CONVENTION

In May 1993, sixty-six countries, including the United States, reached an agreement establishing a cooperative framework between the countries of origin of children in need of adoption and their receiving countries, to ensure that the child's best interests are safeguarded.

The Hague Convention sets minimum international standards and procedures for adoptions that occur between implementing countries. The goal is to protect prospective adoptive children, birth parents and adoptive parents from exploitation. Specifically, the Hague Convention's objectives are to:

1. Prevent abuses such as the abduction or sale of, or the trafficking in, children;

2. Ensure proper consent to the adoption;

3. Allow for the child's transfer to the receiving country; and

4. Establish the adopted child's status in the receiving country.

APPLICABILITY OF HAGUE CONVENTION

The Hague Convention will only apply when the prospective adopted child lives in a country that has implemented the Hague Convention. Such countries are known as "Hague countries." Nevertheless, United States citizens may still adopt a child from any country that allows intercountry adoption.

Further, the Hague Convention will apply not only to children adopted by Americans but also to American children adopted by foreigners. However, it will apply only when both the sending country and the receiving country have implemented the Hague Convention.

HAGUE COUNTRIES

Not every signatory country has yet implemented the Hague Convention on intercountry adoption. As of January 2001, the following countries have implemented the Hague Convention, and are thus considered Hague countries:

Andorra

Australia

Austria

Brazil

Burkina Faso

Burundi

Canada

Chile

Colombia

Costa Rica

Czech Republic

Cyprus

Denmark

Ecuador

El Salvador

Finland

France

Georgia

Iceland

Israel

Italy

Lithuania

Mauritius

Mexico

Moldova

Monaco

Netherlands

New Zealand

Norway

Panama

Paraguay

Peru

Philippines

Poland

Romania

Spain

Sri Lanka

Sweden

Venezuela

Prospective adoptive parents are advised to contact the U.S. Central Authority to obtain current information regarding which countries have implemented the Hague Convention.

DESIGNATED CENTRAL AUTHORITY

Each Hague country must designate a Central Authority to monitor requests for intercountry adoption. The United States Department of State has been designated the U.S. Central Authority for the United States, and its role is to coordinate matters between countries of origin and the United States. The U.S. Central Authority will also control the accreditation of adoption agencies.

AMENDMENTS TO THE IMMIGRATION AND NATIONALITY ACT

The Intercountry Adoption Act amends the Immigration and Nationality Act (INA) by adding two new sections designated Section 101(b)(1)(G) and Section 204(d)(2). However, these two new sections apply only when the child to be adopted resides in a Hague country. A child adopted from a country that has not implemented the Hague Convention will still need to qualify as an orphan or adopted child under Section 101(b)(1)(E) or (F) of the INA.

Section 101(b)(1)(G)

Section 101(b)(1)(G) defines a child as under the age of sixteen at the time an immigrant petition is filed on the child's behalf. The child must be adopted in a foreign state that is a party to the Hague Convention. Alternatively, the child must be emigrating from such a foreign state to be adopted in the United States. In either instance, the prospective adoptive parents must be a United States citizen and spouse jointly, if a married couple, or an unmarried United States citizen at least twenty-five years of age.

This section will also permit the adoption of some children who do not qualify as "orphans" under existing immigration law. However, the adopted child's two living biological parents must be incapable of providing proper care for the child. In addition, they must freely give their written irrevocable consent to terminate their legal relationship with the child, and to allow the child to be adopted and to emigrate.

The written irrevocable consent may also be given by a single parent when the child has one sole or surviving parent because of the death, disappearance, abandonment or desertion by the other parent, by previous adoptive parents, or by other persons or institutions that retain legal custody of the child.

In addition, this section provides that the Attorney General must be satisfied that the purpose of the adoption is to form a bona fide parent-child relationship, and the parent-child relationship of the child and the biological or previous adoptive parents has been terminated.

Section 204(d)(2)

The Hague Convention provides that adoptions between Hague countries may not be completed unless both the sending country and the receiving country have certified that the child will be allowed to immigrate to the country of his or her adoptive parent(s).

Section 204(d)(2) requires the issuance of an adoption or custody certificate by the designated Central Authority for children adopted from Hague countries. This certificate will be conclusive evidence of the relationship between the child being adopted and the adoptive parent, and will help streamline documentary requirements for Hague country adoptions.

Further, the IAA requires that no immigrant petition may be approved on behalf of a child being adopted between two Hague countries unless the Secretary of State has certified that the Central Authority of the child's country of origin has notified the U. S. Central Authority that a United States citizen residing in the United States has effected final adoption of the child, or has been granted custody of the child for the purpose of emigration and adoption.

Thus, when a U.S. citizen adopts a child from a Hague Country, they can be assured that the child will be eligible to immigrate to the United States. This is because adoption in the sending country will not be permitted to take place before the adoption certificate issued by the U.S. Department of State establishes the child's eligibility to immigrate to the United States.

The text of The Intercountry Adoption Act of 2000 is set forth at Appendix 12.

CHAPTER 6:
ADOPTION AGENTS AND FACILITATORS

IN GENERAL

Prospective adoptive parents are encouraged to use the services of a qualified adoption agency for information and guidance on the procedures involved in international adoption and the immigration of the adopted child to the United States. However, prospective adoptive parents are strongly cautioned to seek out a reputable agency with established international adoption experience, and who can provide the parent with competent legal representation.

The local Bureau of Citizenship and Immigration and Services' (BCIS) District Office maintains a list of reputable adoption professionals or agencies that may be able to assist the prospective adoptive parent in locating a child and bringing the child to the United States.

ADOPTION FRAUD—UNITED STATES AGENCIES

International adoptions are a lucrative business, largely due to the unmet demand for adoptable children. Prospective adoptive parents who are emotionally involved in their quest to adopt a child are easy targets of unscrupulous individuals motivated by personal gain. Unscrupulous adoption practitioners are known to entice clients by advertising that they can provide a faster, cheaper, and easier way to adopt children.

Although most adoption practitioners in the United States are legitimate professionals with experience in domestic and international adoptions, some unscrupulous and inexperienced adoption agencies and facilitators have been able to open businesses to purportedly locate children available for adoption, and assist in the adoption process. These agencies often charge the prospective adoptive parents exorbitant fees for services that are never provided.

In addition, two common adoption abuses perpetrated by such agencies include:

1. Knowingly offering a supposedly healthy child for adoption who is later found to be seriously ill; and

2. Obtaining prepayment for adoption of a nonexistent or ineligible child.

This problem is due, in large part, to the lack of regulatory requirements for international adoption agencies in a number of states.

ADOPTION FRAUD—FOREIGN AGENCIES

The U.S. Department of State (DOS) has received a growing number of complaints concerning adoption agencies and facilitators operating in various foreign countries. In some instances, it has been found that foreign children are stolen from their parents for adoption in the United States. There is also a market for fraudulent documents for children who could be beneficiaries of orphan petitions.

The licensing of adoption agencies and facilitators is done in accordance with local law, however, not all foreign governments require that adoption agencies and facilitators be licensed. Thus, it can be difficult to hold unscrupulous adoption facilitators accountable for fraud, malfeasance, or other bad practices in general. The DOS does not, therefore, endorse individual adoption agencies or facilitators in a foreign country.

INVESTIGATION OF ADOPTION PRACTITIONERS

Many of the pitfalls involved in international adoption can be avoided by using reputable adoption agencies, attorneys, and adoption facilitators. The prospective adoptive parent is advised to investigate the background of any persons who will be assisting in the adoption, and ask as many questions as necessary to become completely familiar with the international adoption procedure. If the answers to these important questions appear to be vague, contradictory, or otherwise suspect, this could signal a potential problem.

For example, prospective adoptive parents should question the agency about the qualifications and experience of any facilitators it might use in a foreign country, and the degree to which the agency assumes responsibility for the actions of its agents or facilitators. If the agency asserts that it is not responsible for the actions of its agents or facilitators, this should raise concerns.

Prospective adoptive parents should check with state licensing agencies and consumer protection agencies regarding the qualifications of, and possible complaints against, any adoption agency they are considering. Contact information for state licensing agencies and national adoption organizations is available from the National Adoption Information Clearinghouse (NAIC).

Another way to check the credentials of a prospective adoption practitioner is to ask for their references and contact other adoptive families who have had experience with the particular agency or facilitator. The Better Business Bureau may also be able to provide information as to whether there has been a negative report about a particular adoption agency. However, they do not generally maintain information on individual adoption facilitators.

A directory of national adoption organizations and parent support groups is set forth at Appendix 13.

REPORTING ADOPTION FRAUD

Any encounters with unscrupulous adoption agencies or facilitators should be reported to the appropriate governmental authorities, such as the Bureau of Citizenship and Immigration Services (BCIS), the state Attorney General's office, the District Attorney's Office, the state social services department, etc. Some states have acted to revoke licenses or prosecute the individuals connected with these fraudulent activities after receiving complaints.

ORPHAN INVESTIGATION

The BCIS makes every effort to ensure that an orphan petition does not involve fraudulent adoption practices. Thus, when the BCIS has reason to believe that an orphan petition may involve fraudulent adoption practices, the overseas orphan investigation is done before the petition is approved. This could delay the completion of the case, however, it protects the prospective adoptive parent from the painful ramifications of an invalid adoption.

Sections of law and regulations relating to international adoption which may be of interest to adoptive and prospective adoptive parents, adoption agencies, community-based organizations and attorneys who represent adoptive and prospective adoptive parents are set forth at Appendix 14.

APPENDIX 1:
APPLICATION FOR ADVANCE PROCESSING OF ORPHAN PETITION (FORM I-600A)

OMB No. 1115-0049

U.S. Department of Justice
Immigration and Naturalization Service

Application for Advance Processing of Orphan Petition (8CFR 204.1(b)(3))

Advanced processing is a procedure for completing the part of an orphan petition relating to the petitioner before an orphan is located so that there will be no unnecessary delays in processing the petition after an orphan is located.
USE THIS FORM ONLY IF YOU WISH TO ADOPT AN ORPHAN WHO HAS NOT YET BEEN LOCATED AND IDENTIFIED OR YOU AND/OR YOUR SPOUSE, IF MARRIED, ARE/IS GOING ABROAD TO ADOPT OR LOCATE A CHILD.
This application is not a petition to classify orphan as an immediate relative (Form I-600).

1. Eligibility.

A. Eligibility for advance processing application (Form I-600A). An application for advance processing may be filed by a married United States citizen and spouse. The spouse does not need to be a United States citizen. It may also be filed by an unmarried United States citizen at least 24 years of age provided that he or she will be at least 25 at the time of the adoption and of filing an orphan petition in behalf of a child.

B. Eligibility for Orphan Petition (Form I-600). In addition to the requirements concerning the citizenship and age of the petitioner described in Instruction 1a, when a child is located and identified, the following eligibility requirements will apply:

(1) **Child.** Under immigration law, an orphan is an alien child who has no parents because of the death or disappearance of, abandonment or desertion by, or separation or loss from both parents. An orphan is also a child who has only one parent who is not capable of taking care of the orphan and who has, in writing, irrevocably released the orphan for emigration and adoption. A petition to classify an alien as an orphan may not be filed in behalf of a child in the United States unless that child is in parole status and has not been adopted in the United States. The petition must be filed before the child's 16th birthday.

(2) **Adoption abroad.** If the orphan was adopted abroad, it must be established that both the married petitioner and spouse or the unmarried petitioner personally saw and observed the child prior to or during the adoption proceedings. The adoption decree must show that a married petitioner and spouse adopted the child jointly or that an unmarried petitioner was at least 25 years of age at the time of the adoption.

(3) **Proxy adoption abroad.** If both the petitioner and spouse or the unmarried petitioner did not personally see and observe the child prior to or during the adoption proceedings abroad, the petitioner (and spouse, if married) must submit a statement indicating the petitioner's (and, if married, the spouse's) willingness and intent to readopt the child in the United States. If requested, the petitioner must submit a statement by an official of the state in which the child will reside that readoption is permissible in that state. In addition, evidence of compliance with the preadoption requirements, if any, of that state must be submitted.

(4) **Preadoption requirements.** If the orphan has not been adopted abroad, the petitioner and spouse or the unmarried petitioner must establish that the child will be adopted in the United States by the petitioner and spouse jointly or by the unmarried petitioner and that the preadoption requirement, if any, of the state of the orphan's proposed residence have been met.

2. Filing Advance Processing Application.

An advance processing application must be submitted on Form I-600A with the certification of prospective petitioner executed and the required fee. If the prospective petitioner is married, the Form I-600A must also be signed by the prospective petitioner's spouse. The application must be accompanied by:

A. Proof of United States citizenship of the prospective petitioner.

(1) If the petitioner is a citizen by reason of birth in the United States, submit a copy of the petitioner's birth certificate, or if birth certificate is unobtainable, a copy of petitioner's baptismal certificate under seal of the church, showing place of birth, (baptism must have occurred within two months after birth), or if a birth or baptismal certificate cannot be obtained, affidavits of two United States citizens who have personal knowledge of petitioner's birth in the United States.

(2) If the petitioner was born outside the United States and became a citizen through the naturalization or citizenship of a parent or husband and has not been issued a certificate of citizenship in his or her own name, submit evidence of the citizenship and marriage of the parent or husband, as well as termination of any prior marriages. Also, if petitioner claims citizenship through a parent, submit a copy of the petitioner's birth certificate and a separate statement showing the date, place, and means of all his/her arrivals and departures into and out of the United States.

(3) If petitioner's naturalization occurred within 90 days immediately preceding the filing of this petition, or if it occurred prior to September 27, 1906, a copy of the naturalization certificate must accompany the petition.

(4) An unexpired U.S. passport initially issued for ten years may also be submitted.

B. Proof of marriage of petitioner and spouse.
The married petitioner should submit a copy of the certificate of the marriage and proof of termination of all prior marriages of himself or herself and spouse. In the case of an unmarried petitioner who was previously married, submit proof of termination of all prior marriages. **NOTE:** If any change occurs in the petitioner's marital status while the case is pending, the district director should be notified immediately.

C. A home study with a statement or attachment recommending or approving of the adoption or proposed adoption signed by an official of the responsible state agency in the state of the child's proposed residence or of an agency authorized by that state, or, in the case of a child adopted abroad, of an appropriate public or private adoption agency which is licensed in the United States. Both individuals and organizations may qualify as agencies. If the recommending agency is a licensed agency, the recommendation must set forth that it is licensed, the state in which it is licensed, its license number, if any, and the period of validity of its license. The research, including interviewing, however, and the preparation of the home study may be done by an individual or group in the United States or abroad satisfactory to the recommending agency. A responsible state agency or licensed agency can accept a home study made by an unlicensed or foreign agency and use that home study as a basis for a favorable recommendation. The home study must contain, but is not limited to, the following elements:

(1) the financial ability of the adoptive or prospective parent or parents to rear and educate the child.

(2) a detailed description of the living accommodations where the adoptive or prospective parent or parents currently reside.

(3) A detailed description of the living accommodations where the child will reside.

(4) A factual evaluation of the physical, mental, and moral capabilities of the adoptive or prospective parent or parents in relation to rearing and educating the child.

D. Fingerprints.
Each member of the married prospective adoptive couple or the married prospective adoptive parent, and each additional adult member of the prospective adoptive parents' household must be fingerprinted in connection with this petition.

(1) *Petitioners residing in the United States.* After filing this petition, INS will notify each person in writing of the time and location where they must go to be fingerprinted. Failure to appear to be fingerprinted may result in denial of the petition.

(2) *Petitioners residing Abroad.* Completed fingerprint cards (Forms FD-258)

Form I-600A Instructions (Rev. 12/04/01)Y Page 2

must be submitted with the petition. Do not bend, fold, or crease completed fingerprint cards. Fingerprint cards must be prepared by a United States consular office or a United States military installation.

3. General Filing Instructions.

A. Type or print legibly in ink.

B. If extra space is needed to complete any item, attach a continuation sheet, indicate the item number, and date and sign each sheet.

C. Translations. Any foreign language document must be accompanied by a full English translation, which the translator has certified as complete and correct, and by the translator's certification that he or she is competent to translate the foreign language into English.

D. Copies. If these instructions state that a copy of a document may be filed with this petition and you choose to send us the original, we may keep that original for our records.

4. Submission of Application.

A prospective petitioner residing in the United States should send the completed application to the office of this Service having jurisdiction over his or her place of residence. A prospective petitioner residing outside the United States should consult the nearest American consulate for the overseas or stateside INS office designated to act on the application.

5. Fee. (Read instructions carefully.)

A fee of four hundred and sixty dollars ($460) must be submitted for filing this petition. There is a fifty dollar ($50) per person fingerprinting fee in addition to the petition fee for each person residing in the United States and required to be fingerprinted. For example, if a petition is filed by a married couple residing in the United States with one additional adult member in their household, the total of fees that must be submitted is $610. However, if a petition is filed by a married couple residing abroad, only the petition fee of $460 must be submitted.

One check or money order may be submitted for both the petition fee and the fingerprinting fees. All fees must be submitted in the exact amount. Payment by check or money order must be drawn on a bank or other institution located in the

United States and be payable in United States currency.

If petitioner resides in Guam, the check or money order must be payable to the "Treasurer, Guam."

If petitioner resides in the Virgin Islands, the check or money order must be payable to the "Commissioner of Finance of the Virgin Islands."

All other petitioners must make the check or money order payable to the "Immigration and Naturalization Service." When a check is drawn on the account of a person other than the petitioner, the name of the petitioner must be entered on the face of the check.

If petition is submitted from outside the United States, remittance may be made by bank international money order or foreign draft drawn on a financial institution in the United States and payable to the Immigration and Naturalization Service in United States currency. Personal checks are accepted subject to collectibility. An uncollectible check in payment of a petition fee will render the petition and any document issued invalid. A charge of $30.00 will be imposed if a check in payment of a fee is not honored by the bank on which it is drawn.

When more than one petition is submitted by the same petitioner in behalf of orphans who are siblings, only one set of petition and fingerprinting fees is required.

6. When Child/Children Located and/or Identified.

A separate Form I-600, Petition to Classify Orphan as an Immediate Relative, must be filed for each child. A new fee is not required if only one form I-600 is filed and it is filed within one year of completion of all advance processing in a case where there has been a favorable determination concerning the beneficiary orphan.

Normally, Form I-600 should be submitted to the INS office where the advance processing application was filed. The immigration and Naturalization Service has offices in the following countries: Austria, China, Cuba, Denmark, Domincan Republic, Ecuador, El Salvador, Germany, Ghana, Great Britain, Greece, Guatemala, Haiti, Honduras, India, Italy, Jamaica, Kenya, Korea, Mexico, Pakistan, Panama, Peru, Philippines, Russia, Singapore, South Africa, Spain, Thailand, and Vietnam. A prospective petitioner who is going abroad to adopt or locate a child in one of these countries should file Form I-600 at the INS office having jurisdiction over the place where the child is residing or will be located, unless the case is being retained at the stateside office.

However, a prospective petitioner who is going abroad to any other country to adopt or locate a child should file Form I-600 at the American consulate or embassy having jurisdiction over the place where the child is residing or will be located unless the case is being retained at the stateside office.

The case may be retained at the stateside office, if the petitioner requests it and if it appears that the case will be processed more quickly in that manner. Form I-600 must be accompanied by all the evidence required on the instruction sheet of that form, except that the evidence required by and submitted with this form need not be furnished.

7. **Assistance.**

Assistance may be obtained from a recognized social agency or from any public or private agency. The following recognized social agencies, which have offices in many of the principal cities of the United States, have agreed to furnish assistance:

Bethany Christian Services.
2600 Fivemile Road NE
Grand Rapids, MI. 49525
Tel: (616) 224-7446
Fax: (616) 224-7585

Catholic Legal Immigration Network, Inc. (CLINIC)
415 Michigan Avenue, NE., Suite 150
Washington, DC 20017
Tel: (202) 635-2556
Fax: (202) 632-2649

International Social Services/U.S. of America Branch.
700 Light Street
Baltimore, MD. 21230
Tel: (410) 230-2734
Fax: (410) 230-2741

United States Catholic Conference Migration and Refugee Services (USCC/MRS).
3211 4th Street, NE
Washington, DC 20017
Tel: (202) 541-3352
Fax: (202) 722-8800

8. **Penalties.**
Willful false statements on this form or supporting documents can be punished by fine or imprisonment. U.S. Code, Title 18, Sec. 1001 (Formerly Sec. 80.)

9. **Authority.**
8 U.S.C 1154(a). Routine uses for disclosure under the Privacy Act of 1974 have been published in the Federal Register and are available upon request. The Immigration and Naturalization Service will use the information to determine immigrant eligibility. Submission of the information is voluntary, but failure to provide any or all of the information may result in denial of the petition.

10. **Reporting Burden.**
A person is not required to respond to a collection of information unless it displays a currently valid OMB control number. Public reporting burden for this collection of information is estimated to average 30 minutes per response, including the time for reviewing instructions, searching existing data sources, gathering and maintaining the data needed, and completing and reviewing the collection of information. Send comments regarding this burden estimate or any other aspect of this collection of information, including suggestions for reducing this burden, to: Immigration and Naturalization Service, HQPDI, 425 I Street, N.W., Room 4034, Washington, DC 20536; OMB No. 1115-0049. **DO NOT MAIL YOUR COMPLETED APPLICATION TO THIS ADDRESS.**

Form I-600A Instructions (Rev. 12/04/01)Y Page 4

OMB No. 1115-0049

U.S. Department of Justice
Immigration and Naturalization Service

Application for Advance Processing of Orphan Petition [8CFR 204.1(b)(3)]

Please do not write in this block.

It has been determined that the

☐ Married   ☐ Unmarried

Fee Stamp

There

☐ are   ☐ are not
preadoptive requirements in the state of the child's
proposed residence.

The following is a description of the preadoption requirements, if
any, of the state of the child's proposed residence:

DATE OF FAVORABLE
DETERMINATION

DD

DISTRICT

The preadoption requirements, if any,
☐ have been met.   ☐ have not been met.

File number of petitioner, if applicable

Please type or print legibly in ink.
Application is made by the named prospective petitioner for advance processing of an orphan petition.

BLOCK I - Information about prospective petitioner

1. My name is: (Last)   (First)   (Middle)

2. Other names used (including maiden name if appropriate):

3. I reside in the U.S. at: (C/O if appropriate)   (Apt. No.)

   (Number and street)   (Town or city)   (State)   (ZIP Code)

4. Address abroad (if any):   (Number and street)   (Apt. No.)

   (Town or city)   (Province)   (Country)

5. I was born on: (Month)   (Day)   (Year)

   In: (Town or City)   (State or Province)   (Country)

6. My phone number is: (Include Area Code)

7. My marital status is:
   ☐ Married
   ☐ Widowed
   ☐ Divorced
   ☐ Single

   ☐ I have never been married.
   ☐ I have been previously married _____ time(s).

8. If you are now married, give the following information:
   Date and place of present marriage

   Name of present spouse (include maiden name of wife)

   Date of birth of spouse   Place of birth of spouse

   Number of prior marriages of spouse

   My spouse resides ☐ With me   ☐ Apart from me
                                      (provide address below)
   (Apt. No.)   (No. and street)   (City)   (State)   (Country)

9. I am a citizen of the United States through:
   ☐ Birth   ☐ Parents   ☐ Naturalization
   If acquired through naturalization, give name under which
   naturalized, number of naturalization certificate, and date and
   place of naturalization.

   If not, submit evidence of citizenship. See Instruction 2.a(2).
   If acquired through parentage, have you obtained a certificate
   in your own name based on that acquisition?
   ☐ No   ☐ Yes
   Have you or any person through whom you claimed citizenship
   ever lost United States citizenship?
   ☐ No   ☐ Yes (If yes, attach detailed explanation.)

Continue on reverse.

Received	Trans. In	Ret'd Trans. Out	Completed

Form I-600A (Rev. 12/04/01)Y Page 1

BLOCK II - General information

10. Name and address of organization or individual assisting you in locating or identifying an orphan

(Name)

(Address)

11. Do you plan to travel abroad to locate or adopt a child?
    ☐ Yes   ☐ No

12. Does your spouse, if any, plan to travel abroad to locate or adopt a child?
    ☐ Yes   ☐ No

13. If the answer to question 11 or 12 is "yes," give the following information:

    a. Your date of intended departure _____

    b. Your spouse's date of intended departure _____

    c. City, province _____

14. Will the child come to the United States for adoption after compliance with the preadoption requirements, if any, of the state of proposed residence?
    ☐ Yes   ☐ No

15. If the answer to question 14 is "no," will the child be adopted abroad after having been personally seen and observed by you and your spouse, if married?
    ☐ Yes   ☐ No

16. Where do you wish to file your orphan petition?

    The service office located at

    The American Embassy or Consulate at

17. Do you plan to adopt more than one child?
    ☐ Yes   ☐ No

    If "Yes", how many children do you plan to adopt?

Certification of prospective petitioner

I certify, under penalty of perjury under the laws of the United States of America, that the foregoing is true and correct and that I will care for an orphan/orphans properly if admitted to the United States.

(Signature of Prospective Petitioner)

Executed on (Date)

Certification of married prospective petitioner's spouse

I certify, under penalty of perjury under the laws of the United States of America, that the foregoing is true and correct and that my spouse and I will care for an orphan/orphans properly if admitted to the United States.

(Signature of Prospective Petitioner)

Executed on (Date)

Signature of person preparing form, if other than petitioner

I declare that this document was prepared by me at the request of the prospective petitioner and is based on all information of which I have any knowledge.

(Signature)

Address

Executed on (Date)

Form I-600A (Rev. 12/04/01)Y Page 2

APPENDIX 2:
APPLICATION FOR ACTION ON AN
APPROVED APPLICATION OR PETITION
(FORM I-824)

OMB No. 1115-0176

| U.S. Department of Justice | Application for Action on an Approved |
| Immigration and Naturalization Service | Application or Petition |

START HERE - Please Type or Print (Instructions on back)

FOR INS USE ONLY

Part 1. Information about the person that filed the original application or petition. (Individuals should use the top name line; Organizations should use the second line.)

Family Name		Given Name		Middle Initial

Company or Organization Name

Address - Attn:

Street Number and Name			Apt #
City		State or Province	
Country		Zip/Postal Code	

Date of Birth (Month/Day/Year)		Country of Birth	
Social Security #	IRS Tax #	A #	

For INS Use Only column:

Returned	Receipt
Resubmitted	
Reloc Sent	
Reloc Rec'd	

Part 2. Application type (check one).

a. ☐ I am applying for a duplicate approval notice.

b. ☐ I am requesting that a new U.S. Consulate or Port of Entry be notified of the previous approval of a petition. Please notify the new U.S. Consulate or Port of Entry at:

c. ☐ I am requesting that a U.S. Consulate be notified that my status has been adjusted to permanent resident. Please notify the U.S. Consulate at:

☐ Applicant Interviewed

☐ Duplicate Notice
☐ American Consulate Notified at (Location):
☐ Application Denied

Action Block

Part 3. Processing information.

Type of Petition/ Application (Form #)	Filing Receipt #
Date of Filing (Month/Day/Year)	Date Approved (Month/Day/Year)

If the petition is filed for another person, give the following about the person you filed for:

Family Name		Given Name		Middle Initial
Date of Birth (Month/Day/Year)		Country of Birth		
A#				

To Be Completed by Attorney or Representative, if any
☐ Fill in box if G-28 is attached to represent the applicant

VOLAG#

ATTY State License #

Part 4. Signature Read the information on penalties in the instructions before completing this section.

I certify, under penalty of perjury under the laws of the United States of America, that this application and the evidence submitted with it is all true and correct. I authorize the release of any information from my records which the Immigration and Naturalization Service needs to determine eligibility for the benefit I am seeking.

Signature	Date
Print Your Name	

Form I-824 (Rev. 12-05-01)Y

APPLICATION FOR ACTION ON AN APPROVED APPLICATION OR PETITION

Part 5. Signature of person preparing form, if other than above. *(Sign Below)*

I declare that I prepared this application at the request of the above person and it is based on information of which I have knowledge.

Signature	Print Your Name	Date
Firm Name and Address		

Purpose of This Form.
This form is used to request further action on a previously approved petition or application.

Who May File.
If you filed an application or petition which has been approved, use this form during the validity of the approved application or petition to:

- request a duplicate approval notice;
- request that another U.S.Embassy or consulate be notified of the approval of the petition; or
- request that a U.S. Embassy or consulate be notified that your status has been adjusted to permanent resident, so your spouse and children can apply for immigrant visas.

You should enclose a copy of the original approval notice. It may speed processing.

General Filing Instructions.
Please answer all questions by typing or clearly printing in black ink. Indicate that an item is not applicable with "N/A." If an answer is "none," write "none." If you need extra space to answer any item, attach a sheet of paper with your name and your alien registration number (A#), if any, and indicate the number of the item to which the answer refers. Your application must be properly signed and filed with the correct fee. If you are under 14 years of age, your parent or guardian may sign the application.

Where to File.
File this application with the INS Service Center or office that approved the original application or petition.

Fee.
The fee for this application is $140.00. The fee must be submitted in the exact amount. It cannot be refunded. **DO NOT MAIL CASH.**

All checks and money orders must be drawn on a bank or other institution located in the United States and must be payable in United States currency. The check or money order should be made payable to the Immigration and Naturalization Service, except that:

- if you live in Guam, make your check or money order payable to the "Treasurer, Guam."
- if you live in the Virgin Islands and are filing this application in the Virgin Islands, make your check or money order payable to the "Commissioner of Finance of the Virgin Islands."

Checks are accepted subject to collection. An uncollected check will render the application and any document issued invalid. A charge of $30.00 will be imposed if a check in payment of a fee is not honored by the bank on which it is drawn.

Processing Information.
Acceptance. Any application that is not signed or is not accompanied by the correct fee will be rejected with a notice that the application is deficient. You may correct the deficiency and resubmit the application. However, an application is not considered properly filed until accepted by the INS.

Initial processing. Once the application has been accepted, it will be checked for completeness. If you do not completely fill out the form, you will not establish a basis for eligibility, and we may deny your application.

Requests for more information or interview. We may request more information or evidence or we may request that you appear at an INS office for an interview. We may also request that you submit the originals of any copy. We will return these originals when they are no longer required.

Decision. You will be notified in writing of the decision on your application.

Penalties.
If you knowingly and willfully falsify or conceal a material fact or submit a false document with this request, we will deny the benefit you are seeking and may deny any other immigration benefit. In addition, you will face severe penalties provided by law, and may be subject to criminal prosecution.

Privacy Act Notice.
We ask for the information on this form, and associated evidence to determine if you have established eligibility for the immigration benefit you are seeking. Our legal right to ask for this information is in 8 USC 1103. We may provide this information to other government agencies. Failure to provide this information and any requested evidence, may delay a final decision or result in denial of your request.

Paperwork Reduction Act Notice.
An agency may not conduct or sponsor an information collection and a person is not required to respond to an informaiton collection unless it displays a currently valid OMB control number. The estimated average time to complete and file this application is as follows: (1) 5 minutes to learn about the law and form; (2) 5 minutes to complete the form; and (3) 15 minutes to assemble and file the application; for a total estimated average of 25 minutes per application. If you have comments regarding the accuracy of this estimate, or suggestions for making this form simpler, you can write to the Immigration and Naturalization Service, HQPDI, 425 I Street, N.W., Room 4034, Washington DC, 20536; OMB No. 1115-0176. **DO NOT MAIL YOUR COMPLETED APPLICATION TO THIS ADDRESS.**

APPENDIX 3:
PETITION TO CLASSIFY ORPHAN AS IMMEDIATE RELATIVE
(FORM I-600)

OMB NO. 1115-0049

U.S. Department of Justice
Immigration and Naturalization Service

Petition to Classify Orphan as an Immediate Relative

1. Eligibility.

A. Child. Under immigration law, an orphan is an alien child who has no parents because of the death or disappearance of, abandonment or desertion by, or separation or loss from both parents. An orphan is also a child who has only one parent who is not capable of taking care of the orphan and who has, in writing, irrevocably released the orphan for emigration and adoption. A petition to classify an alien as an orphan may not be filed in behalf of a child in the United States, unless that child is in parole status and has not been adopted in the United States. The petition must be filed before the child's 16th birthday.

B. Parent(s). The petition may be filed by a married United States citizen and spouse or unmarried United States citizen at least twenty-five years of age. The spouse does not need to be a United States citizen.

C. Adoption abroad. If the orphan was adopted abroad, it must be established that both the married petitioner and spouse or the unmarried petitioner personally saw and observed the child prior to or during the adoption proceedings. The adoption decree must show that a married petitioner and spouse adopted the child jointly or that an unmarried petitioner was at least 25 years of age at the time of the adoption.

D. Proxy adoption abroad. If both the petitioner and spouse or the unmarried petitioner did not personally see and observe the child prior to or during the adoption proceedings abroad, the petitioner (and spouse, if married) must submit a statement indicating the petitioner's (and, if married, the spouse's) willingness and intent to readopt the child in the United States. If requested, the petitioner must submit a statement by an official of the state in which the child will reside that readoption is permissible in that state. In addition, evidence of compliance with the preadoption requirements, if any, of that state must be submitted.

E. Preadoption requirements. If the orphan has not been adopted abroad, the petitioner and spouse or the unmarried petitioner must establish that the child will be adopted in the United States by the petitioner and spouse jointly or by the unmarried petitioner and that the preadoption requirement, if any, of the state of the orphan's proposed residence have been met.

2. Filing petition for known child.

An orphan petition for a child who has been identified must be submitted on a completed Form I-600 with the certification of petitioner executed and the required fee. If the petitioner is married, the Form I-600 must also be signed by the petitioner's spouse. The petition must be accompanied by the following:

A. Proof of United States citizenship of the petitioner.

(1) If the petitioner is a citizen by reason of birth in the United States, submit a copy of the petitioner's birth certificate, or if birth certificate is unobtainable, a copy of petitioner's baptismal certificate under the seal of the church, showing place of birth, (baptism must have occurred within two months after birth), or if a birth or baptismal certificate cannot be obtained, affidavits of two United States citizens who have personal knowledge of petitioner's birth in the United States.

(2) If the petitioner was born outside the United States and became a citizen through the naturalization or citizenship of a parent or husband and has not been issued a certificate of citizenship in his or her own name, submit evidence of the citizenship and marriage of the parent or husband, as well as termination of any prior marriages.

Form I-600 Instructions (Rev. 11/28/01)Y

Also, if petitioner claims citizenship through a parent, submit petitioner's birth certificate and a separate statement showing the date, place, and means of all his or her arrivals and departures into and out of the United States.

(3) If petitioner's naturalization occurred within 90 days immediately preceding the filing of this petition, or if it occurred prior to September 27, 1906, the naturalization certificate must accompany the petition.

(4) An unexpired U.S. passport initially issued for ten years may also be submitted.

B. **Proof of marriage of petitioner and spouse.**
The married petitioner should submit a certificate of the marriage and proof of termination of all prior marriages of himself or herself and spouse. In the case of an unmarried petitioner who was previously married, submit proof of termination of all prior marriages. **NOTE:** If any change occurs in the petitioner's marital status while the case is pending, the district director should be notified immediately.

C. **Proof of age of orphan.**
Petitioner should submit a copy of the orphan's birth certificate if obtainable; if not obtainable, submit an explanation together with the best available evidence of birth.

D. **Copies of the death certificate(s) of the child's parent(s), if applicable.**

E. **A certified copy of adoption decree together with certified translation,** if the orphan has been lawfully adopted abroad.

F. **Evidence that the sole or surviving parent is incapable of providing for the orphan's care** and has, in writing, irrevocably released the orphan for emigration and adoption, if the orphan has only one parent.

G. **Evidence that the orphan has been unconditionally abandoned to an orphanage,** if the orphan has been placed in an orphanage by his/her parent or parents.

H. **Evidence that the preadoption requirements, if any, of the state of the orphan's proposed residence have been met,** if the child is to be adopted in the United States. If it is not possible to submit this evidence upon initial filing of the petition under the laws of the state of proposed residence, it may be submitted later. The petition, however, will not be approved without it.

I. **A home study** with a statement or attachment recommending or approving of the adoption or proposed adoption signed by an official of the responsible state agency in the state of the child's proposed residence or of an agency authorized by that state, or, in the case of a child adopted abroad, of an appropriate public or private adoption agency which is licensed in the United States. Both individuals and organizations may qualify as agencies. If the recommending agency is a licensed agency, the recommendation must set forth that it is licensed, the state in which it is licensed, its license number, if any, and the period of validity of its license. The research, including interviewing, however, and the preparation of the home study may be done by an individual or group in the United States or abroad satisfactory to the recommending agency. A responsible state agency or licensed agency can accept a home study made by an unlicensed agency. An unlicensed agency can accept a home study made by an unlicensed or foreign agency and use that home study as a basis for a favorable recommendation. The home study must contain, but is not limited to, the following elements:

(1) the financial ability of the adoptive or prospective parent or parents to read and educate the child.

(2) a detailed description of the living accommodations where the adoptive or prospective parent or parents currently reside.

(3) a detailed description of the living accommodations where the child will reside.

(4) a factual evaluation of the physical, mental, and moral capabilities of the adoptive or prospective parent or parents in relation to rearing and educating the child.

Form I-600 Instructions (Rev.11/28/01)Y Page 2

J. Fingerprints.
Each member of the married prospective adoptive couple or the married prospective adoptive parent, and each additional adult member of the prospective adoptive parents' household must be fingerprinted in connection with this petition.

Petitioners residing in the United States. After filing this petition, INS will notify each person in writing of the time and location where they must go to be fingerprinted. Failure to appear to be fingerprinted may result in denial of the petition.

Petitioners residing abroad. Completed fingerprint cards (Forms FD-258) must be submitted with the petition. Do not bend, fold, or crease completed fingerprint cards. Fingerprint cards must be prepared by a United States consular office or a United States military installation.

3. **Filing Petition for Known Child Without Full Documentation on Child or Home Study.**
When a child has been identified but the documentary evidence relating to him/her or the home study is not yet available, an orphan petition may be filed without that evidence or home study. The evidence outlined in Instructions 2A and 2B, however, must be submitted. If the necessary evidence relating to the child or the home study is not submitted within one year from the date of submission of the petition, the petition will be considered abandoned and the fee will not be refunded. Any further proceeding will require the filing of a new petition.

4. **Submitting an Application for Advance Processing of an Orphan Petition in Behalf of a Child Who Has Not Been Identified.**
A prospective petitioner may request advance processing when the child has not been identified or when the prospective petitioner and/or spouse are or is going abroad to locate or adopt a child. If unmarried, the prospective petitioner must be at least 24 years of age, provided that he or she will be at least 25 at the time of the adoption and the completed petition in behalf of a child is filed. The request must be on Form I-600A, Application for Advance Processing of Orphan Petition, and must be accompanied by the evidence required by that form. After a child or children are located and/or identified, a separate Form I-600, Petition to Classify Orphan as an Immediate Relative, must be filed for each child. A new fee is not required if only one Form I-600 is filed, provided the form is filed within one year of completion of all advance

processing in a case where there has been a favorable determination concerning the prospective petitioner's ability to care for a beneficiary orphan.

5. **When Child/Children Located and/or Identified.**
A separate form I-600, Petition to Classify Orphan as an Immediate Relative, must be filed for each child. A new fee is not required if only one form I-600 is filed and it is filed within one year of completion of all advance processing in a case where there has been a favorable determination concerning the beneficiary orphan.

Normally, Form I-600 should be submitted to the INS office where the advance processing application was filed. The Immigration and Naturalization Service has offices in the following countries: Austria, China, Cuba, Denmark, Dominican Republic, Ecuador, El Salvador, Germany, Ghana, Great Britain, Greece, Guatemala, Haiti, Honduras, India, Italy, Jamaica, Kenya, Korea, Mexico, Pakistan, Panama, Peru, Philippines, Russia, Singapore, South Africa, Spain, Thailand, and Vietnam. A prospective petitioner who is going abroad to adopt or locate a child in one of these countries should file Form I-600 at the INS office having jurisdiction over the place where the child is residing or will be located unless the case is being retained at the stateside office.

However, a prospective petitioner who is going abroad to any other country to adopt or locate a child should file Form I-600 at the American embassy or consulate having jurisdiction over the place where the child is residing or will be located unless the case is being retained at the stateside office.

The case may be retained at the stateside office, if the petitioner requests it and if it appears that the case will be processed more quickly in that manner. Form I-600 must be accompanied by all the evidence required on the instruction sheet of that form, except that the evidence required by and submitted with this form need not be furnished.

6. **General Filing Instructions.**

A. Type or print legibly in ink.

B. If extra space is needed to complete any item, attach a continuation sheet, indicate the item number, and date and sign each sheet.

C. **Translations.** Any foreign language document must be accompanied by a full English translation, which the translator has certified as complete and correct, and by the translator's certification that he or she is competent to translate the foreign language into English.

D. **Copies.** If these instruction state that a copy of a document may be filed with this petition and you choose to send us the original, we may keep that original for our records.

7. Submission of petition.

A petitioner residing in the United States should send the completed petition to the INS office having jurisdiction over his/her place of residence. A petitioner residing outside the United States should consult the nearest American embassy or consulate designated to act on the petition.

8. Fee. Read instructions carefully.

A fee of four hundred and sixty dollars ($460) must be submitted for filing this petition. There is a fifty dollar ($50) per person, fingerprinting fee, in addition to the petition fee for each person residing in the United States and required to be fingerprinted. For example, if a petition is filed by a married couple residing in the United States with one additional adult member in their household, the total of fees that must be submitted is $610. However, if a petition is filed by a married couple residing abroad, only the petition fee of $460 must be submitted.

One check or money order may be submitted for both the petition fee and the fingerprinting fees. It cannot be refunded regardless of the action taken on the petition. **Do not mail cash. All fees must be submitted in the exact amount.** Payment by a check or money order must be drawn on a bank or other institution located in the United States and be payable in United States currency.

If the petitioner resides in Guam, the check or money order must be payable to the "Treasurer, Guam."

If the petitioner resides in the Virgin Islands, check or money order must be payable to the "Commissioner of Finance of the Virgin Islands."

All other petitioners must make the check or money order payable to the "Immigration and Naturalization Service." When a check is drawn on the account of a person other than the petitioner, the name of the petitioner must be entered on the face of the check.

If petition is submitted from outside the United States, remittance may be made by a bank international money order or foreign draft drawn on a financial institution in the United States and payable to the Immigration and Naturalization Service in United States currency. Personal checks are accepted subject to collectibility. An uncollectible check in payment of a petition fee will render the petition and any document issued invalid. A charge of $30.00 will be imposed if a check in payment of a fee is not honored by the bank on which it is drawn. When more than one petition is submitted by the same petitioner in behalf of orphans who are siblings, only one set of petition and fingerprinting fees is required.

9. Assistance.

Assistance may be obtained from a recognized social agency or from any public or private agency. The following recognized social agencies, which have offices in many of the principal cities of the United States, have agreed to furnish assistance:

Bethany Christian Services.
2600 Fivemile Road NE
Grand Rapids, MI. 419525
Tel: (616) 224-7446
Fax: (616) 224-7585

Catholic Legal Immigration Network, Inc., (CLINIC).
415 Michigan Avenue, NE., Suite 150
Washington, DC 20017
Tel: (202) 635-2556
Fax: (202) 635-2649

International Social Services/U.S. of America Branch
700 Light Street
Baltimore, MD. 21230
Tel: (410) 230-2734
Fax: (410) 230-2741

United States Catholic Conference Migration and Refugee Services (USCC/MRS).
3211 4th Street, NE
Washington, DC 20017
Tel: (202) 541-3352
Fax: (202) 722-8800

10. Penalties.

Willful false statements on this form or supporting documents can be punished by fine or imprisonment. U.S. Code, Title 18, Sec. 1001 (formerly Sec. 80.)

Form I-600 Instructions (Rev. 11/28/01)Y Page 4

11 Authority.

8 USC 1154(a). Routine uses for disclosure under the Privacy Act of 1974 have been published in the Federal Register and are available upon request. INS will use the information to determine immigrant eligibility. Submission of the information is voluntary, but failure to provide any or all of the information may result in denial of the petition.

12 Reporting Burden.

A person is not required to respond to a collection of information unless it displays a currently valid OMB control number. Public reporting burden for this collection of information is estimated to average 30 minutes per response, including the time for reviewing instructions, searching existing data sources, gathering and maintaining the data needed, and completing and reviewing the collection of information. Send comments regarding this burden estimate or any other aspect of this collection of information, including suggestions for reducing this burden, to: Immigration and Naturalization Service, HQPDI, 425 I Street, N.W., Room 4034, Washington, DC 20536; OMB No. 1115-0049. **DO NOT MAIL YOUR COMPLETED APPLICATION TO THIS ADDRESS.**

OMB No. 1115-0049

Petition to Classify Orphan as an Immediate Relative

U.S. Department of Justice
Immigration and Naturalization Service

[Section 101 (b)(1)(F) of the Immigration and Nationality Act, as amended.]

Please do not write in this block.

TO THE SECRETARY OF STATE;
The petition was filed by:

☐ Married petitioner   ☐ Unmarried petitioner

The petition is approved for orphan:

☐ Adopted abroad   ☐ Coming to U.S. for adoption. Preadoption requirements have been met.

Remarks:

Fee Stamp

File number

DATE OF ACTION

DD

DISTRICT

Please type or print legibly in ink. Use a separate petition for each child.

Petition is being made to classify the named orphan as an immediate relative.

BLOCK I - Information about prospective

1. My name is: (Last)   (First)   (Middle)

2. Other names used (including maiden name if appropriate):

3. I reside in the U.S.   (C/O if appropriate)   (Apt. No.)

   (Number and street)   (Town or city)   (State)   (Zip Code)

4. Address abroad (if any)(Number and street)   (Apt. No.)

   (Town or city)   (Province)   (Country)

5. I was born on: (Month)   (Day)   (Year)

   In: (Town or City)   (State or Province)   (Country)

6. My phone number is: (Include Area Code)

7. My marital status is:
   ☐ Married
   ☐ Widowed
   ☐ Divorced
   ☐ Single
       ☐ I have never been married.
       ☐ I have been previously married _____ time(s).

8. If you are now married, give the following information:

   Date and place of present marriage

   Name of present spouse (include maiden name of wife)

   Date of birth of spouse   Place of birth of spouse

   Number of prior marriages of spouse

   My spouse resides ☐ With me   ☐ Apart from me
                                        (provide address below)
   (Apt. No.)   (No. and street)   (City)   (State)   (Country)

9. I am a citizen of the United States through:
   ☐ Birth   ☐ Parents   ☐ Naturalization

   If acquired through naturalization, give name under which naturalized, number of naturalization certificate, and date and place of naturalization:

   If not, submit evidence of citizenship. See Instruction 2.a(2).

   If acquired through parentage, have you obtained a certificate in your own name based on that acquisition?
   ☐ No   ☐ Yes

   Have you or any person through whom you claimed citizenship ever lost United States citizenship?
   ☐ No   ☐ Yes (If yes, attach detailed explanation.)

Continue on reverse.

Received	Trans. In	Ret'd Trans. Out	Completed

Form I-600 (Rev. 11/28/01)Y Page 1

BLOCK II - Information about orphan beneficiary

10. Name at birth   (First)   (Middle)   (Last)

20. To petitioner's knowledge, does the orphan have any physical or affliction? ☐ Yes   ☐ No

    If "Yes", name the affliction.

11. Name at present   (First)   (Middle)   (Last)

12. Any other names by which orphan is or was known.

21. Who has legal custody of the child?

13. Sex ☐ Male   ☐ Female
14. Date of birth (Month/Day/Year)

22. Name of child welfare agency, if any, assisting in this case:

15. Place of birth (City)   (State or Province)   (Country)

23. Name of attorney abroad, if any, representing petitioner in this

    Address of above.

16. The beneficiary is an orphan because (check One)
    ☐ He/she has no parents.
    ☐ He/she has only one parent who is the sole or surviving

24. Address in the United States where orphan will reside.

17. If the orphan has only one parent, answer the following
    a. State what has become of the other parent:

25. Present address of orphan.

    b. Is the remaining parent capable of providing for the orphan's support? ☐ Yes   ☐ No
    c. Has the remaining parent, in writing, irrevocably released orphan for emigration and adoption? ☐ Yes   ☐ No

25. If orphan is residing in an institution, give full name of institution.

18. Has the orphan been adopted abroad by the petitioner and jointly or the unmarried petitioner? ☐ Yes   ☐ No

    If yes, did the petitioner and spouse or unmarried petitioner personally see and observe the child prior to or during the adoption proceedings? ☐ Yes   ☐ No

    Date of adoption

    Place of adoption

26. If orphan is not residing in an institution, give full name of person whom orphan is residing.

27. Give any additional information necessary to locate orphan such as name of district, section, zone or locality in which orphan resides.

19. If either answer in question 18 is "No", answer the following:
    a. Do petitioner and spouse jointly or does the unmarried intend to adopt the orphan in the United States?
       ☐ Yes   ☐ No
    b. Have the preadoption requirements, if any, of the orphan's proposed state of residence been met?
       ☐ Yes   ☐ No
    c. If b. is answered "No", will they be met later?
       ☐ Yes   ☐ No

28. Location of American Consulate where application for visa will be made.
    (City in Foreign Country)   (Foreign Country)

Certification of prospective petitioner

I certify under penalty of perjury under the laws of the United States of America that the foregoing is true and correct and that I will care for an orphan/orphans properly if admitted to the United States.

(Signature of Prospective Petitioner)

Executed on (Date)

Certification of married prospective petitioner's spouse

I certify under penalty of perjury under the laws of the United States of America that the foregoing is true and correct and that my spouse and I will care for an orphan/orphans properly if admitted to the United States.

(Signature of Prospective Petitioner)

Executed on (Date)

Signature of person preparing form, if other than petitioner

I declare that this document was prepared by me at the request of the prospective petitioner and is based on all information of which I have any knowledge.

(Signature)

Address

Executed on (Date)

Form I-600 (Rev. 11/28/01)Y Page 2

APPENDIX 4:
NOTICE OF APPEAL TO THE
ADMINISTRATIVE APPEALS UNIT
(FORM 1290B)

U.S. Department of Justice
Immigration and Naturalization Service

Notice of appeal to the
Administrative Appeals Unit (AAU)

Important: See instructions on other side.

Fee Stamp

In the Matter of:

File Number:

1. I am filing an appeal from the decision dated:

2. Please check the one block which applies:

☐ I am not submitting a separate brief or evidence.

☐ I am submitting a separate brief and/or evidence with this form.

☐ I am sending a brief and/or evidence to the AAU within 30 days

☐ I need _____ days to submit a brief and/or evidence to the AAU.   *(May be granted only for good cause shown. Explain in a separate letter.)*

Person Filing Appeal

SIGNATURE _____

Name _____

Address _____
    Number   *Street*

_____
   City   *State*   *ZIP Code*

Date _____

☐ I am an attorney or representative, and I represent:

Person and/or organization for whom you are appearing

You must attach a Notice of Entry of Appearance (Form G-28) if you are an attorney or representative and did not submit such a form before.

3. Briefly, state the reason(s) for this appeal:

Form 1290B(Rev. 01/04/91)N

U.S. Department of Justice
Immigration and Naturalization Service

Notice of appeal to the
Administrative Appeals Unit (AAU)

INSTRUCTIONS

1. **Filing.** You must file your appeal with the Immigration and Naturalization Service (INS) office which made the unfavorable decision within 30 calendar days after service of the decision (33 days if your decision was mailed). The date of service is normally the date of the decision. Do _not_ send your appeal directly to the Administrative Appeals Unit (AAU). Submit an original appeal only. Additional copies are not required.

2. **Fee.** You must pay $110.00 to file this form. (You only need to pay one fee of $110.00 if two or more aliens are covered by the unfavorable decision.) **The fee will not be refunded, regardless of the action taken in your case.** DO NOT MAIL CASH. all checks or money orders, whether U.S. or foreign, must be payable in U.S. currency at a financial institution in the United States. When a check is drawn on the account of a person other than yourself. write your name on the face of the check. If the check is not honored, INS will charge you $5.00.

   Pay by check or money order in the exact amount. Make the check or money order payable to "Immigration and Naturalization Service." However,

   A. if you live in Guam, make the check or money order payable to "Treasurer, Guam," or

   B. if you live in the U.S. Virgin Islands. make the check or money order payable to "Commissioner of Finance of the Virgin Islands."

3. **Attorney or Representative.** You may. if you wish, be represented. at no expense to the government, by an attorney or other duly authorized representative. Notice of Entry of Appearance (Form G-28)that your attorney or representative must submit with this notice is available at INS offices.

4. **Brief.** You do not need to submit a brief in support of your appeal, but you may submit one. Or you may submit a simple written statement instead. You may also submit evidence.

   You may submit a brief, statement, and/or evidence _with_ this form. Or you may send these materials to the AAU within 30 days of the date you sign this form. You must send any materials you submit _after_ filing the appeal to:

   > Administrative Appeals Unit
   > Immigration and Naturalization Service
   > 425 Eye Street, N.W.
   > Washington, D.C. 20536

   If you need more than 30 days, you must explain why in a separate letter attached to this form. The AAU may grant more time _only_ for good cause.

5. **Oral Argument.** You may ask for oral argument before the AAU in Washington, D.C., in a separate letter attached to this form. The letter must explain specifically why oral argument is necessary.

   If your request is granted. the AAU will write to you about setting the date and time. Oral argument is normally limited to fifteen minutes. The government does not furnish interpreters for oral argument.

6. **Visa Petition Beneficiary.** If you are the beneficiary of a visa petition or the beneficiary's attorney or representative you may _not_ file an appeal on this form. When a decision on a petition may be appealed, the petitioner, an authorized official of a petitioning corporation, or the petitioner's attorney or representative must sign this form. (The only exceptions are the beneficiaries of third preference and Public Law 97-359 Amerasian petitions. These beneficiaries may file appeals on this form.)

Form I290B (Rev. 01/04/91)N

APPENDIX 5:
TABLE OF NUMBER OF IMMIGRANT VISAS ISSUED TO ORPHANS COMING TO THE UNITED STATES, WORLD TOTAL (CALENDAR YEARS 1989-2002)

YEAR	NUMBER OF VISAS
1989	8,102
1990	7,093
1991	8,481
1992	6,472
1993	7,377
1994	8,333
1995	8,987
1996	10,641
1997	12,743
1998	15,774
1999	16,363
2000	17,718
2001	19,237
2002	20,099

Source: United States Department of State.

APPENDIX 6:
TABLE OF NUMBER OF IMMIGRANT VISAS ISSUED TO ORPHANS COMING TO THE UNITED STATES, TOP TWENTY COUNTRIES OF ORIGIN (2001)

COUNTRY	NUMBER OF VISAS
CHINA (mainland)	4681
RUSSIA	4279
SOUTH KOREA	1870
GUATEMALA	1609
UKRAINE	1246
ROMANIA	782
VIETNAM	737
KAZAKHSTAN	672
INDIA	543
COLOMBIA	407
BULGARIA	297
CAMBODIA	266
PHILIPPINES	219
HAITI	192
ETHIOPIA	158
BELARUS	129
POLAND	86
THAILAND	74
MEXICO	73

COUNTRY	NUMBER OF VISAS
JAMAICA	51
LIBERIA	51

Source: United States Department of State.

APPENDIX 7:
TABLE OF NUMBER OF IMMIGRANT VISAS ISSUED TO ORPHANS COMING TO THE UNITED STATES, TOP TWENTY COUNTRIES OF ORIGIN (2002)

COUNTRY	NUMBER OF VISAS
CHINA (mainland)	5053
RUSSIA	4939
GUATEMALA	2219
SOUTH KOREA	1779
UKRAINE	1106
KAZAKHSTAN	819
VIETNAM	766
INDIA	466
COLOMBIA	334
BULGARIA	260
CAMBODIA	254
PHILIPPINES	221
HAITI	187
BELARUS	169
ROMANIA	168
ETHIOPIA	105
POLAND	101
THAILAND	67
PERU	65

COUNTRY	NUMBER OF VISAS
MEXICO	61

Source: United States Department of State.

APPENDIX 8:
AFFIDAVIT CONCERNING EXEMPTION FROM IMMIGRANT VACCINATION REQUIREMENTS FOR A FOREIGN ADOPTED CHILD (FORM DS-1981)

U.S Department of State
Affidavit Concerning Exemption from Immigrant
Vaccination Requirements for a Foreign Adopted Child

Statement for Parent(s): Section 212(a)(1)(A)(ii) of the Immigration and Nationality Act requires that any person who seeks admission as an immigrant, or adjustment of status to the status of an alien lawfully admitted for permanent residence, shall present documentation of having received vaccination against vaccine-preventable diseases, specifically: mumps, measles, rubella, polio, tetanus and diphtheria toxoids, pertussis, influenze type B, hepatitis B, varicella and pneumoccocal. This section exempts from the immunization requirement a child who:

      (i) is 10 years of age or younger;
      (ii) is described in Section 101(b)(1)(F), and
      (iii) is seeking an immigrant visa as an immediate relative under section 201(b),

provided that the adoptive parent or prospective adoptive parent, prior to the child's admission, executes an affidavit stating that the parent is aware of the provisions of subparagraph (A)(ii) and will ensure that, within 30 days of the child's admission, or at the earliest time that is medically appropriate, the child will receive the vaccinations identified in such subparagraph.

Section 101(b)(1) defines the term "child" as an unmarried person under twenty-one years of age. **Subparagraph (F)** refers to a child, under the age of sixteen at the time a petition is filed in his behalf to accord classification as an immediate relative under section 201(b), who is an orphan because of the death or disappearance of, abandonment or desertion by, or separation or loss from, both parents, or for whom the sole surviving parent is incapable of providing the proper care and has in writing irrevocably released the child for emigration and adoption; who has been adopted abroad by a United States citizen and spouse jointly, or by an unmarried United States citizen at least twenty-five years of age, who personally saw and observed the child prior to or during the adoption proceedings; or who is coming to the United States for adoption by a United States citizen and spouse jointly, or by an unmarried United States citizen at least twenty-five years of age, who have or has complied with the preadoption requirements, if any, of the child's proposed residence: Provided, that the Attorney General is satisfied that proper care will be furnished the child if admitted to the United States: Provided further, that no natural parent or prior adoptive parent of any such child shall thereafter, by virtue of such parentage, be accorded any right, privilege, or status under this Act.

Affidavit by Adoptive Parent or Prospective Adoptive Parent

I, _____ , certify that I am the adoptive parent/prospective adoptive
parent of a child, _____ , on whose behalf I have filed or will file an
I-600 *(petition to classify orphan as immediate relative)* according said child status as an orphan as defined by Section 101(b)(1)(F).

I have read the statement above and I am aware of the vaccination requirement set forth in Section 212(a)(1)(A)(ii) of the Immigration and Nationality Act. In accordance with Section 212(a)(1)(A)(ii), I will ensure that my foreign adopted child receives the required and medically appropriate vaccinations within 30 days after his or her admission into the U.S., or at the earliest time that is medically appropriate.

Signed this _____ day of _____ , _____ , at _____ .

_____
(Signature of Parent)

Subscribed and sworn to *(or affirmed)* before me this _____ day of _____ , _____
at _____ . My commission expires on *(mm-dd-yyyy)* _____

_____
(Signature of Notary Public or Officer Administering Oath)

DS-1981
06-2000

APPENDIX 9:
THE CHILD CITIZENSHIP ACT OF 2000

PUBLIC LAW 106-395—106TH CONGRESS

An Act

To amend the Immigration and Nationality Act to modify the provisions governing acquisition of citizenship by children born outside of the United States, and for other purposes.

Be it enacted by the Senate and House of Representatives of the United States of America in Congress assembled,

SECTION 1. SHORT TITLE.

This Act may be cited as the "Child Citizenship Act of 2000".

TITLE I—CITIZENSHIP FOR CERTAIN CHILDREN BORN OUTSIDE THE UNITED STATES

SEC. 101. AUTOMATIC ACQUISITION OF CITIZENSHIP FOR CERTAIN CHILDREN BORN OUTSIDE THE UNITED STATES.

(a) IN GENERAL—Section 320 of the Immigration and Nationality Act (8 U.S.C. 1431) is amended to read as follows:

"children born outside the united states and residing permanently in the united states; conditions under which citizenship automatically acquired

"SEC. 320. (a) A child born outside of the United States automatically becomes a citizen of the United States when all of the following conditions have been fulfilled:

"(1) At least one parent of the child is a citizen of the United States, whether by birth or naturalization.

"(2) The child is under the age of eighteen years.

"(3) The child is residing in the United States in the legal and physical custody of the citizen parent pursuant to a lawful admission for permanent residence.

"(b) Subsection (a) shall apply to a child adopted by a United States citizen parent if the child satisfies the requirements applicable to adopted children under section 101(b)(1).".

(b) CLERICAL AMENDMENT—The table of sections of such Act is amended by striking the item relating to section 320 and inserting the following:

"Sec. 320. Children born outside the United States and residing permanently in the United States; conditions under which citizenship automatically acquired.".

SEC. 102. ACQUISITION OF CERTIFICATE OF CITIZENSHIP FOR CERTAIN CHILDREN BORN OUTSIDE THE UNITED STATES.

(a) IN GENERAL—Section 322 of the Immigration and Nationality Act (8 U.S.C. 1433) is amended to read as follows:

"children born and residing outside the united states; conditions for acquiring certificate of citizenship

"SEC. 322. (a) A parent who is a citizen of the United States may apply for naturalization on behalf of a child born outside of the United States who has not acquired citizenship automatically under section 320. The Attorney General shall issue a certificate of citizenship to such parent upon proof, to the satisfaction of the Attorney General, that the following conditions have been fulfilled:

"(1) At least one parent is a citizen of the United States, whether by birth or naturalization.

"(2) The United States citizen parent—

"(A) has been physically present in the United States or its outlying possessions for a period or periods totaling not less than five years, at least two of which were after attaining the age of fourteen years; or

"(B) has a citizen parent who has been physically present in the United States or its outlying possessions for a period or periods totaling not less than five years, at least two of which were after attaining the age of fourteen years.

"(3) The child is under the age of eighteen years.

"(4) The child is residing outside of the United States in the legal and physical custody of the citizen parent, is temporarily present in the United States pursuant to a lawful admission, and is maintaining such lawful status.

"(b) Upon approval of the application (which may be filed from abroad) and, except as provided in the last sentence of section 337(a), upon taking and subscribing before an officer of the Service within the United States to the oath of allegiance required by this Act of an applicant for naturalization, the child shall become a citizen of the United States and shall be furnished by the Attorney General with a certificate of citizenship.

"(c) Subsections (a) and (b) shall apply to a child adopted by a United States citizen parent if the child satisfies the requirements applicable to adopted children under section 101(b)(1).".

(b) CLERICAL AMENDMENT—The table of sections of such Act is amended by striking the item relating to section 322 and inserting the following:

"Sec. 322. Children born and residing outside the United States; conditions for acquiring certificate of citizenship.".

SEC. 103. CONFORMING AMENDMENT.

(a) IN GENERAL—Section 321 of the Immigration and Nationality Act (8 U.S.C. 1432) is repealed.

(b) CLERICAL AMENDMENT—The table of sections of such Act is amended by striking the item relating to section 321.

SEC. 104. EFFECTIVE DATE.

The amendments made by this title shall take effect 120 days after the date of the enactment of this Act and shall apply to individuals who satisfy the requirements of section 320 or 322 of the Immigration and Nationality Act, as in effect on such effective date.

TITLE II—PROTECTIONS FOR CERTAIN ALIENS VOTING BASED ON REASONABLE BELIEF OF CITIZENSHIP

SEC. 201. PROTECTIONS FROM FINDING OF BAD MORAL CHARACTER, REMOVAL FROM THE UNITED STATES, AND CRIMINAL PENALTIES.

(a) PROTECTION FROM BEING CONSIDERED NOT OF GOOD MORAL CHARACTER—

(1) IN GENERAL—Section 101(f) of the Immigration and Nationality Act (8 U.S.C. 1101(f)) is amended by adding at the end the following:

"In the case of an alien who makes a false statement or claim of citizenship, or who registers to vote or votes in a Federal, State, or local election (including an initiative, recall, or referendum) in violation of a lawful restriction of such registration or voting to citizens, if each natural parent of the alien (or, in the case of an adopted alien, each adoptive parent of the alien) is or was a citizen (whether by birth or naturalization), the alien permanently resided in the United States prior to attaining the age of 16, and the alien reasonably believed at the time of such statement, claim, or violation that he or she was a citizen, no finding that the alien is, or was, not of good moral character may be made based on it.".

(2) EFFECTIVE DATE—The amendment made by paragraph (1) shall be effective as if included in the enactment of the Illegal Immigration Reform and Immigrant Responsibility Act of 1996 (Public Law 104-208; 110 Stat. 3009-546) and shall apply to individuals having an application for a benefit under the Immigration and Nationality Act pending on or after September 30, 1996.

(b) PROTECTION FROM BEING CONSIDERED INADMISSIBLE—

(1) UNLAWFUL VOTING—Section 212(a)(10)(D) of the Immigration and Nationality Act (8 U.S.C. 1182(a)(10)(D)) is amended to read as follows:

"(D) UNLAWFUL VOTERS—

"(i) IN GENERAL—Any alien who has voted in violation of any Federal, State, or local constitutional provision, statute, ordinance, or regulation is inadmissible.

"(ii) EXCEPTION—In the case of an alien who voted in a Federal, State, or local election (including an initiative, recall, or referendum) in violation of a lawful restriction of voting to citizens, if each natural parent of the alien (or, in the case of an adopted alien, each adoptive parent of the alien) is or was a citizen (whether by birth or naturalization), the alien permanently resided in the United States prior to attaining the age of 16, and the alien reasonably believed at the time of such violation that he or she was a citizen, the alien shall not be considered to be inadmissible under any provision of this subsection based on such violation.".

(2) FALSELY CLAIMING CITIZENSHIP—Section 212(a)(6)(C)(ii) of the Immigration and Nationality Act (8 U.S.C. 1182(a)(6)(C)(ii)) is amended to read as follows:

"(ii) FALSELY CLAIMING CITIZENSHIP—

"(I) IN GENERAL—Any alien who falsely represents, or has falsely represented, himself or herself to be a citizen of the United States for any purpose or benefit under this Act (including section 274A) or any other Federal or State law is inadmissible.

"(II) EXCEPTION—In the case of an alien making a representation described in subclause (I), if each natural parent of the alien (or, in the case of an adopted alien, each adoptive parent of the alien) is or was a citizen (whether by birth or naturalization), the alien permanently resided in the United States prior to attaining the age of 16, and the alien reasonably believed at the time of making such representation that he or she was a citizen, the alien shall not be considered to be inadmissible under any provision of this subsection based on such representation.".

(3) EFFECTIVE DATES—The amendment made by paragraph (1) shall be effective as if included in the enactment of section 347 of the Illegal Immigration Reform and Immigrant Responsibility Act of 1996 (Public Law 104-208; 110 Stat. 3009-638) and shall apply to voting occurring before, on, or after September 30, 1996. The amendment made by paragraph (2) shall be effective as if included in the enactment of section 344 of the Illegal Immigration Reform and Immigrant Responsibility Act of 1996 (Public Law 104-208; 110 Stat. 3009-637) and shall apply to representations made on or after September 30, 1996. Such amendments shall apply to individuals in proceedings under the Immigration and Nationality Act on or after September 30, 1996.

(c) PROTECTION FROM BEING CONSIDERED DEPORTABLE—

(1) UNLAWFUL VOTING—Section 237(a)(6) of the Immigration and Nationality Act (8 U.S.C. 1227(a)(6)) is amended to read as follows:

"(6) UNLAWFUL VOTERS—

"(A) IN GENERAL—Any alien who has voted in violation of any Federal, State, or local constitutional provision, statute, ordinance, or regulation is deportable.

"(B) EXCEPTION—In the case of an alien who voted in a Federal, State, or local election (including an initiative, recall, or referendum) in violation of a lawful restriction of voting to citizens, if each natural parent of the alien (or, in the case of an adopted alien, each adoptive parent of the alien) is or was a citizen (whether by birth or naturalization), the alien permanently resided in the United States prior to attaining the age of 16, and the alien reasonably believed at the time of such violation that he or she was a citizen, the alien shall not be considered to be deportable under any provision of this subsection based on such violation.".

(2) FALSELY CLAIMING CITIZENSHIP—Section 237(a)(3)(D) of the Immigration and Nationality Act (8 U.S.C. 1227(a)(3)(D)) is amended to read as follows:

"(D) FALSELY CLAIMING CITIZENSHIP—

"(i) IN GENERAL—Any alien who falsely represents, or has falsely represented, himself to be a citizen of the United States for any purpose or benefit under this Act (including section 274A) or any Federal or State law is deportable.

"(ii) EXCEPTION—In the case of an alien making a representation described in clause (i), if each natural parent of the alien (or, in the case of an adopted alien, each adoptive parent of the alien) is or was a citizen (whether by birth or naturalization), the alien permanently resided in the United States prior to attaining the age of 16, and the alien reasonably believed at the time of making such representation that he or she was a citizen, the alien shall not be considered to be deportable under any provision of this subsection based on such representation.".

(3) EFFECTIVE DATES—The amendment made by paragraph (1) shall be effective as if included in the enactment of section 347 of the Illegal Immigration Reform and Immigrant Responsibility Act of 1996 (Public Law 104-208; 110 Stat. 3009-638) and shall apply to voting occurring before, on, or after September 30, 1996. The amendment made by paragraph (2) shall be effective as if included in the enactment of section 344 of the Illegal Immigration Reform and Immigrant Responsibility Act of 1996 (Public Law 104-208; 110 Stat. 3009-637) and shall apply to representations made on or after September 30, 1996. Such amendments shall apply to individuals in proceedings under the Immigration and Nationality Act on or after September 30, 1996.

(d) PROTECTION FROM CRIMINAL PENALTIES—

(1) CRIMINAL PENALTY FOR VOTING BY ALIENS IN FEDERAL ELECTION—Section 611 of title 18, United States Code, is amended by adding at the end the following:

"(c) Subsection (a) does not apply to an alien if—

"(1) each natural parent of the alien (or, in the case of an adopted alien, each adoptive parent of the alien) is or was a citizen (whether by birth or naturalization);

"(2) the alien permanently resided in the United States prior to attaining the age of 16; and

"(3) the alien reasonably believed at the time of voting in violation of such subsection that he or she was a citizen of the United States.".

(2) CRIMINAL PENALTY FOR FALSE CLAIM TO CITIZENSHIP—Section 1015 of title 18, United States Code, is amended by adding at the end the following:

> "Subsection (f) does not apply to an alien if each natural parent of the alien (or, in the case of an adopted alien, each adoptive parent of the alien) is or was a citizen (whether by birth or naturalization), the alien permanently resided in the United States prior to attaining the age of 16, and the alien reasonably believed at the time of making the false statement or claim that he or she was a citizen of the United States.".

(3) EFFECTIVE DATES—The amendment made by paragraph (1) shall be effective as if included in the enactment of section 216 of the Illegal Immigration Reform and Immigrant Responsibility Act of 1996 (Public Law 104-208; 110 Stat. 3009-572). The amendment made by paragraph (2) shall be effective as if included in the enactment of section 215 of the Illegal Immigration Reform and Immigrant Responsibility Act of 1996 (Public Law 104-208; 110 Stat. 3009-572). The amendments made by paragraphs (1) and (2) shall apply to an alien prosecuted on or after September 30, 1996, except in the case of an alien whose criminal proceeding (including judicial review thereof) has been finally concluded before the date of the enactment of this Act.

APPENDIX 10:
APPLICATION FOR CERTIFICATE OF CITIZENSHIP ON BEHALF OF AN ADOPTED CHILD (FORM N-643)

OMB# 1115-0152

U.S. Department of Justice
Immigration and Naturalization Service

Application for Certificate of Citizenship in Behalf of an Adopted Child

INSTRUCTIONS

Who may file? To use this form, you must be a United States citizen and the parent of an adopted child who was born outside the United States. Your spouse (if any) must also be a United States citizen and also the child's adoptive parent. The child must be under 18 years of age and residing with you in the United States as a lawfully admitted permanent resident alien. The approval of this application before the child's 18th birthday will make the child a United States citizen as of the date the application is approved. You will receive a certificate of citizenship as proof of the child's citizenship.

What is the fee? You must pay $145.00 to file this form. The fee will not be refunded. Do not mail cash. All checks or money orders must be payable in the U.S. currency in the United States. Make check or money order payable to "Immigration and Naturalization Service" in the exact amount. If the check is not honored, INS will charge you an additional $30.00.

If you live in Guam and are filing this application in Guam, make your check payable to "Treasurer, Guam," or if you live in the U.S. Virgin Islands and are filing this application there, make it payable to "Commissioner of Finance of the Virgin Islands."

What photographs are needed? You must send three identical, unglazed photographs of the child taken within 30 days of the date of filing of this application. The photographs must be in natural color and taken without a hat. The dimensions of the face should be about 1 inch from the top of the hair to the chin. The face should be a 3/4 frontal view with the entire right ear visible. They must be on thin paper with a light background and not mounted in any way. The photographs must not be signed but you should print the child's name and alien registration number in the center of the back of each photograph in pencil.

What documents are needed?.

- Child's Alien Registration Card.
- Child's Birth Certificate.
- Final adoption decree.
- If the child's name has been legally changed since entry, submit evidence of the name change if not included in the adoption decree.
- Evidence of U.S. citizenship of adoptive parent(s). Submit your birth certificate, if born in the United States; your naturalization certificate, if naturalized; your certificate of citizenship or FS-240 (Report of Birth Abroad of United States Citizen). In place of any of the aforementioned, you may submit your valid, unexpired U.S. passport.

- Marriage certificate of adoptive parents.
- If either of the adoptive parents has been previously married, submit evidence of termination of all prior marriages.

Any document in a foreign language must be accompanied by a translation in English. The translator must certify that he or she is competent to translate and that the translation is accurate.

What if a document is not available? If the documents needed are not available you may submit the following (INS may require a certification from the appropriate civil authority that the document is not available):

- Church record: A certificate under the church seal issued within two months of birth.
- School record: A letter from authorities of the school attended.
- Census records: State or Federal census record.
- Affidavits: Written statements sworn (or affirmed) to by two persons who have personal knowledge of the claimed event.

For each document needed, you may submit the original documents or a clear, readable copy (INS may still require the originals).

Where should the application be filed?

Submit this application at the local INS office having jurisdiction over your place of residence.

What are the penalties for submitting false information? Title 18 United States Code, Section 1001, states that whoever willfully and knowingly falsifies a material fact, makes a false statement, or makes use of a false document will be fined up to $10,000 or imprisoned up to five years or both. In addition, civil penalties may be imposed in accordance with Title 8 United States Code, Section 1324(a)(2).

What is the authority for collecting this information? Information on this form is requested to carry out the immigration laws contained in Title 8 United States Code 1304(c). This information is needed to determine whether an applicant is eligible for immigration benefits. The information provided may also be disclosed to other federal, state, local, and foreign law enforcement and regulatory agencies during the course of the investigation required by this Service. It is not necessary to provide this information, however, if you refuse, your application may be denied.

Paperwork Reduction Act Notice. Under the Paperwork Reduction Act, an agency may not conduct or sponsor an information collection and a person is not required to respond to an information collection unless it displays a currently valid OMB control number. We try to create forms and instructions which are accurate, can be easily understood and which impose the least possible burden on you. Often this is difficult because some immigration laws are very complex. The estimated average time to complete and file this application is as follows: (1) 15 minutes to learn the law and form; (2) 20 minutes to complete the form; and (3) 30 minutes to assemble and file the petition, for a total estimated average of 1 hour and 5 minutes per petition. If you have comments regarding the accuracy of this estimate, or suggestions for making this form simpler, you can write to the Immigration and Naturalization Service, 425 I Street, NW, Room 4034, Washington DC 20536; OMB No. 1115-0152. DO NOT MAIL YOUR COMPLETED APPLICATION TO THIS ADDRESS.

Form N-643 (12/06/01)Y Page1

U.S. Department of Justice
Immigration and Naturalization Service

OMB No. 1115-0152

Certificate of Citizenship on Behalf of Adopted Child

START HERE - Please Type or Print	FOR INS USE ONLY	
Part Information about adopted child.	Returned	Receipt

Last Name	First	Middle

Address:

Resubmitted

Street Number		Apt. #

City	State or Province
Country	ZIP/Postal Code

Reloc Sent

Date of Birth (Mo/Day/Yr)	Place of Birth (City, Country)
Social Security #	A#

Reloc Rec'd

Personal Description:

Sex ☐ Male ☐ Female	Height Ft. _____ In. _____
Marital Status	Visible Marks or Scars

☐ Applicant Interviewed

Information about Entry:

Action Block

Name at Entry (If different from Item A)

Recommendation of Officer:

Date of Entry	Place of Entry

☐ Approval   ☐ Denial

Date of Adoption (Mo/Day/Yr)	Place of Adoption (City, Country)

Part B. Information about the Adoptive Parents (if there is only one parent write "None" in place of the name of the parent which does not apply.)

Last Name of Adoptive Father	First	Middle

U.S. Citizen by: ☐ Birth in the U.S.

Concurrence of District Director or Officer in Charge:

☐ Birth abroad to USC parents (List certificate of citizenship number or passport number)

☐ I do   ☐ do not   ☐ concur

☐ Naturalized or derived after birth (List naturalization certificate number)

Signature

Last Name of Adoptive Mother	First	Middle and Maiden

Certificate # _____

U.S. Citizen by: ☐ Birth in the U.S.

To Be Completed by Attorney or Representative, if any

☐ Birth abroad to USC parents (List certificate of citizenship number or passport number)

☐ Fill in box if G-28 is attached to represent the applicant

☐ Naturalized or derived after birth (List naturalization certificate number)

VOLAG#

ATTY State License #

Form N-643 (12/06/01) Y - Page 2

Part B. *Continued.*

Date and Place of Marriage of the Adoptive Parents

Number of Prior Marriages of Adoptive Father	Number of Prior Marriages of Adoptive Mother

Is residence of parents' the same as the child's?   ☐ YES   ☐ NO   (If no, explain on a separate sheet of paper.)

If the residence address is different from Item A, list actual residence address.   Daytime Telephone #

Part C.   Signature. (Read the information on penalties in the instructions before completing this section.)

I certify that this application, and the evidence submitted with it, is true and correct. I authorize the release of any information from my records, or that of my child which the Immigration and Naturalization Service needs to determine eligibility for the benefit I am seeking.

Signature	*Print Name*	*Date*

Part D.   Signature of person preparing form, if other than above. *(Sign below)*

I declare that I prepared this application at the request of the above person and it is based on all information of which I have knowledge.

Signature	*Print Name*	*Date*

Firm Name
and Address

DO NOT COMPLETE THE FOLLOWING UNTIL INSTRUCTED TO DO SO AT THE INTERVIEW

AFFIDAVIT. I, the (parent, guardian) _____ do swear or affirm, under penalty of the perjury laws of the United States, that I know and understand the contents of this application signed by me, and the attached supplementary pages numbered ( ) to ( ) inclusive; that the same are true and correct to the best of my knowledge, and that corrections numbered ( ) to ( ) were made by me or at my request.

Signature of parent or guardian _____   Date _____

Person Examined	Address	Relationship to Applicant

Sworn or affirmed before me on _____ at _____

Signature of interviewing officer _____ Title _____

Form N-643 (12/06/01) Y- Page 3

APPENDIX 11:
APPLICATION FOR TRANSMISSION OF CITIZENSHIP THROUGH A GRANDPARENT (FORM N-643-SUPP. A)

OMB No. 1115-0203

U.S. Department of Justice
Immigration and Naturalization Service

Application for Transmission of Citizenship Through a Grandparent

Part A.   INSTRUCTIONS
This is a supplement for Forms N-600 and N-643. Attach the completed supplement *(Printed or typed in black or blue ink)* to your Form N-600 or Form 643 and take or mail the application to the appropriate INS office in the United States. *(See reverse for more instructions)*

Part B.   INFORMATION ABOUT CHILD *(PRINT OR TYPE)*

Last Name	First Name	Middle Name	Date of Birth *(Month/Day/Year)*

As a United States citizen parent, I am applying for a certificate of citizenship for my child through his or her *(check appropriate box)*

☐ Grandfather   ☐ Grandmother

Part C.   INFORMATION ABOUT GRANDFATHER *(PRINT OR TYPE)*

Grandfather's Last Name	First Name	Middle Name	Date of Birth *(Month/Day/Year)*

Place of Birth *(City/State/Country)* _____   He currently resides at *(Street Address/City/State/Country)* *(If Deceased, So State)* _____

He became a citizen of the United States by: ☐ Birth ☐ Naturalization ☐ Derivation On *(Month/Day/Year):* _____
In the *(Name of Court, City, State)* _____, Certificate of Naturalization Number: _____
Or through his parent(s), and ☐ was ☐ was not issued a Certificate of Citizenship. If issued provide Number A or AA _____. His former Alien Registration Number was _____. He ☐ has ☐ has not lost United States citizenship. *(If citizenship lost, attach full explanation)* He resided in the United States from *(Year)* _____
to *(Year)* _____; from *(Year)* _____ to *(Year)* _____; from *(Year)* _____ to *(Year)* _____.

Part D.   INFORMATION ABOUT GRANDMOTHER *(PRINT OR TYPE)*

Grandmother's Last Name	First Name	Middle Name	Date of Birth *(Month/Day/Year)*

Place of Birth *(City/State/Country)* _____   She currently resides at *(Street Address/City/State/Country)* *(If Deceased, So State)* _____

She became a citizen of the United States ☐ Birth ☐ Naturalization ☐ Derivation On *(Month/Day/Year):* _____
In the *(Name of Court, City, State)* _____, Certificate of Naturalization Number: _____
Or through her parent(s), and ☐ was ☐ was not issued a Certificate of Citizenship. If issued provide Number A or AA _____. Her former Alien Registration Number was _____. She ☐ has ☐ has not lost United States citizenship. *(If citizenship lost, attach full explanation)* She resided in the United States from *(Year)* _____
to *(Year)* _____; from *(Year)* _____ to *(Year)* _____; from *(Year)* _____ to *(Year)* _____.

My child's grandparents were married to each other on _____ at _____
(Month/Day/Year)   *(City/State/County/Country)*

I certify, under penalty of perjury under the laws of the United States of America, that this application, and the evidence submitted with it, are all true and correct. I authorize the release of any information from my records which the Immigration and Naturalization Service needs to determine eligibility for the benefit I am seeking.

Signature	Print Your Name	Date

Form N-600/N-643 Supplement A (Rev. 05/04/00)Y

INSTRUCTIONS
READ INSTRUCTIONS BEFORE COMPLETING FORM ON REVERSE SIDE
ATTACH FORM TO N-600 OR N-643 APPLICATION

A United States citizen parent (the applicant) should complete this supplement when applying for expeditious naturalization for his or her natural child of Form N-600 or for his or her adopted child on Form N-643. Pursuant to the transmission requirements of section 322 of the Immigration and Nationality Act, the citizen parent must have 5 years physical presence in the United States or its outlying possessions with at least 2 years occurring after age 14, in order to transmit citizenship. Section 322 allows a citizen parent who is unable to transmit citizenship to apply for a certificate of citizenship for his or her child, based on the physical presence of the child's United States citizen grandparent (the United States citizen parent of the applicant).

The parent should document that he and she meets the transmission requirements on a separate paper(s) and attach the documentation to the N-600 or N-643 application. When the parent uses the grandparent's physical presence to meet transmission requirements, he or she should attach this supplement to the N-600 or N-643 application. The grandparent may be living or deceased at the time of application.

Only United States citizen parent may file the N-600 and N-643 application and supplement for his or her child. In the case of divorce, only the citizen parent having legal custody of the child may file the N-600 and N-643 applications and supplement.

If the citizen parent and child live abroad, the N-600 or N-643 application and supplement may be filed at any Immigration and Naturalization Service (INS) District or Sub Office in the United States or its outlying possessions (including San Juan, P.R., the U.S. Virgin Islands, and Guam) or with such other Service office as the Commissioner may designate. If the citizen parent and child reside in the United States, the application and supplement must be filed at the INS office having jurisdiction over the parent's residence.

Both the applicant and child must appear in person for an interview with INS. The applicant must file a separate application and supplement for each child seeking a certificate of citizenship.

The INS will issue a certificate of citizenship to a child whose grandparent meets the transmission requirements when the applicant submits proof of the following: (1) at least one parent is a citizen of the United States, whether by birth, naturalization, or derivation; (2) the child is physically present in the United States pursuant to a lawful admission; (3) the child is under the age of 18 years and in the legal custody of the citizen parent; and (4) if the citizen parent is an adoptive parent of the child, the child was adopted by the citizen parent before the child reached the age of 16 years and the child has been in the legal custody of, and has resided with, adoptive parent or parents for at least two years, or the child is the beneficiary of an orphan petition.

AGE OF APPLICANT: The application must be filed, adjudicated, and approved with the oath of allegiance administered (unless waived) before the child's 18th birthday.

NAME TO BE SHOWN ON CERTIFICATE OF CITIZENSHIP: INS will issue the certificate only in the name the child has the legal right to use. INS cannot authorize name changes.

DOCUMENTS: The applicant must attach a full English translation to any document written in foreign language. The translator must certify that he or she is competent to translate and that the translation is accurate.

REQUIRED DOCUMENTATION: INS will return the entire application packet to the applicant if it does not include the proper documents. The required documents are:

- birth certificates (and naturalization certificates if applicable) of the applicant, child, and grandparent.
- marriage certificate (if the applicant is the child's father) or documents verifying legitimation according to the laws of child's residence.
- legal custody documentation if the applicant is divorced from the child's other parent.

If the applicant's name has been legally changed from what is shown on any birth certificate and/or naturalization or citizenship certificate to be submitted, the applicant must attach the document(s) authorizing the name change, such as a marriage certificate or a court order. Likewise, if the grandparent's name has been legally changed from what is shown on any birth certificate and/or naturalization or citizenship certificate to be submitted, applicant must attach the document(s) authorizing the name change.

The applicant must submit documentation that proves the transmitting grandparent meets the required physical residence period in the United States. The grandparent must have lived in the United States or its outlying possessions for 5 years, at least 2 of those years occurring after the age of 14. Documents may include school records, military records, utility bills, medical records, deeds, mortgages, contracts, insurance policies, receipts, or attestations by churches, unions, or other organizations. If no documents are available the applicant may submit notarized affidavits of at least two persons who were living at the time, and have personal knowledge, of the event described. The person executing the affidavit must state how knowledge of the event was obtained.

The applicant may submit copies of documents rather than originals. If originals are submitted, INS may keep them for their files. If copies are submitted, the applicant should be prepared to present originals at time of the interview.

PRIVACY ACT NOTICE: The Authority to collect this information is contained in Title 8, United States Code. Furnishing the information on this form is voluntary, however, failure to provide all of the requested information may result in the delay of a final decision or denial of your request. The information collected will be used to make a determination on your application. It may, however, be provided to other government agencies (Federal, state, local and/or foreign).

REPORTING BURDEN: A person is not required to respond to a collection of information unless it displays a currently valid OMB control number. We try to create forms and instructions that are accurate, can be easily understood, and which impose the least possible burden on you to provide us with information. Often this is difficult because some immigration laws are very complex. Accordingly, the reporting burden for this collection of information is computed as follows: 1) learning about the form, 11 minutes; 2) completing the form, 7 minutes; and 3) assembling and filing the application, 12 minutes, for an estimated average of 30 minutes per response. If you have comments regarding the accurancy of this estimate, or suggestions for making this form simpler, you can write to the Immigration and Naturalization Service, HQPDI, 425 I Street, N.W., Room 4034, Washington DC 20536, OMB No. 1115-0203. **DO NOT MAIL YOUR COMPLETED APPLICATION TO THIS ADDRESS.**

Form N-600/643 Supplement A (Rev. 05/04/00)Y Page 3

APPENDIX 12:
THE INTERCOUNTRY ADOPTION
ACT OF 2000

H.R. 2909 - 106TH CONGRESS

An Act

To provide for implementation by the United States of the Hague Convention on Protection of Children and Co-operation in Respect of Intercountry Adoption, and for other purposes.

Be it enacted by the Senate and House of Representatives of the United States of America in Congress assembled,

SECTION 1. SHORT TITLE; TABLE OF CONTENTS.

(a) SHORT TITLE—This Act may be cited as the "Intercountry Adoption Act of 2000"

(b) TABLE OF CONTENTS—The table of contents of this Act is as follows:

TITLE II—PROVISIONS RELATING TO ACCREDITATION AND APPROVAL

Sec. 201. Accreditation or approval required in order to provide adoption services in cases subject to the Convention.

Sec. 202. Process for accreditation and approval; role of accrediting entities.

Sec. 203. Standards and procedures for providing accreditation or approval.

Sec. 204. Secretarial oversight of accreditation and approval.

Sec. 205. State plan requirement.

TITLE III—RECOGNITION OF CONVENTION ADOPTIONS IN THE UNITED STATES

Sec. 301. Adoptions of children immigrating to the United States.

Sec. 302. Immigration and Nationality Act amendments relating to children adopted from Convention countries.

Sec. 303. Adoptions of children emigrating from the United States.

TITLE IV—ADMINISTRATION AND ENFORCEMENT

Sec. 401. Access to Convention records.

Sec. 402. Documents of other Convention countries.

Sec. 403. Authorization of appropriations; collection of fees.

Sec. 404. Enforcement.

TITLE V—GENERAL PROVISIONS

Sec. 501. Recognition of Convention adoptions.

Sec. 502. Special rules for certain cases.

Sec. 503. Relationship to other laws.

Sec. 504. No private right of action.

Sec. 505. Effective dates; transition rule.

SEC. 2. FINDINGS AND PURPOSES.

(a) FINDINGS—Congress recognizes—

(1) the international character of the Convention on Protection of Children and Co-operation in Respect of Intercountry Adoption (done at The Hague on May 29, 1993); and

(2) the need for uniform interpretation and implementation of the Convention in the United States and abroad, and therefore finds that enactment of a Federal law governing adoptions and prospective adoptions subject to the Convention involving United States residents is essential.

(b) PURPOSES—The purposes of this Act are—

(1) to provide for implementation by the United States of the Convention;

(2) to protect the rights of, and prevent abuses against, children, birth families, and adoptive parents involved in adoptions (or prospective adoptions) subject to the Convention, and to ensure that such adoptions are in the children's best interests; and

(3) to improve the ability of the Federal Government to assist United States citizens seeking to adopt children from abroad and residents of other countries party to the Convention seeking to adopt children from the United States.

SEC. 3. DEFINITIONS.

As used in this Act:

(1) ACCREDITED AGENCY—The term "accredited agency" means an agency accredited under title II to provide adoption services in the United States in cases subject to the Convention.

(2) ACCREDITING ENTITY—The term "accrediting entity" means an entity designated under section 202(a) to accredit agencies and approve persons under title II.

(3) ADOPTION SERVICE—The term "adoption service" means—

(A) identifying a child for adoption and arranging an adoption;

(B) securing necessary consent to termination of parental rights and to adoption;

(C) performing a background study on a child or a home study on a prospective adoptive parent, and reporting on such a study;

(D) making determinations of the best interests of a child and the appropriateness of adoptive placement for the child;

(E) post-placement monitoring of a case until final adoption; and

(F) where made necessary by disruption before final adoption, assuming custody and providing child care or any other social service pending an alternative placement. The term "providing', with respect to an adoption service, includes facilitating the provision of the service.

(4) AGENCY—The term "agency" means any person other than an individual.

(5) APPROVED PERSON—The term "approved person" means a person approved under title II to provide adoption services in the United States in cases subject to the Convention.

(6) ATTORNEY GENERAL—Except as used in section 404, the term "Attorney General" means the Attorney General, acting through the Commissioner of Immigration and Naturalization.

(7) CENTRAL AUTHORITY—The term "central authority" means the entity designated as such by any Convention country under Article 6(1) of the Convention.

(8) CENTRAL AUTHORITY FUNCTION—The term "central authority function" means any duty required to be carried out by a central authority under the Convention.

(9) CONVENTION—The term "Convention" means the Convention on Protection of Children and Co-operation in Respect of Intercountry Adoption, done at The Hague on May 29, 1993.

(10) CONVENTION ADOPTION—The term "Convention adoption" means an adoption of a child resident in a foreign country party to the Convention by a United States citizen, or an adoption of a child resident in the United States by an individual residing in another Convention country.

(11) CONVENTION RECORD—The term "Convention record" means any item, collection, or grouping of information contained in an electronic or physical document, an electronic collection of data, a photograph, an audio or video tape, or any other information storage medium of any type whatever that contains information about a specific past, current, or prospective Convention adoption (regardless of whether the adoption was made final) that has been preserved in accordance with section 401(a) by the Secretary of State or the Attorney General.

(12) CONVENTION COUNTRY—The term "Convention country" means a country party to the Convention.

(13) OTHER CONVENTION COUNTRY—The term "other Convention country" means a Convention country other than the United States.

(14) PERSON—The term "person" shall have the meaning provided in section 1 of title 1, United States Code, and shall not include any agency of government or tribal government entity.

(15) PERSON WITH AN OWNERSHIP OR CONTROL INTEREST—The term "person with an ownership or control interest" has the meaning given such term in section 1124(a)(3) of the Social Security Act (42 U.S.C. 1320a-3).

(16) SECRETARY—The term "Secretary" means the Secretary of State.

(17) STATE—The term "State" means the 50 States, the District of Columbia, the Commonwealth of Puerto Rico, the Commonwealth of the Northern Mariana Islands, Guam, and the Virgin Islands.

TITLE I—UNITED STATES CENTRAL AUTHORITY

SEC. 101. DESIGNATION OF CENTRAL AUTHORITY.

(a) IN GENERAL—For purposes of the Convention and this Act—

(1) the Department of State shall serve as the central authority of the United States; and

(2) the Secretary shall serve as the head of the central authority of the United States.

(b) PERFORMANCE OF CENTRAL AUTHORITY FUNCTIONS—

(1) Except as otherwise provided in this Act, the Secretary shall be responsible for the performance of all central authority functions for the United States under the Convention and this Act.

(2) All personnel of the Department of State performing core central authority functions in a professional capacity in the Office of Children's Issues shall have a strong background in consular affairs, personal experience in international adoptions, or professional experience in international adoptions or child services.

(c) AUTHORITY TO ISSUE REGULATIONS—Except as otherwise provided in this Act, the Secretary may prescribe such regulations as may be necessary to carry out central authority functions on behalf of the United States.

SEC. 102. RESPONSIBILITIES OF THE SECRETARY OF STATE.

(a) LIAISON RESPONSIBILITIES—The Secretary shall have responsibility for—

(1) liaison with the central authorities of other Convention countries; and

(2) the coordination of activities under the Convention by persons subject to the jurisdiction of the United States.

(b) INFORMATION EXCHANGE—The Secretary shall be responsible for—

(1) providing the central authorities of other Convention countries with information concerning—

(A) accredited agencies and approved persons, agencies and persons whose accreditation or approval has been suspended or canceled, and agencies and persons who have been temporarily or permanently debarred from accreditation or approval;

(B) Federal and State laws relevant to implementing the Convention; and

(C) any other matters necessary and appropriate for implementation of the Convention;

(2) not later than the date of the entry into force of the Convention for the United States (pursuant to Article 46(2)(a) of the Convention) and at least once during each subsequent calendar year, providing to the central authority of all other Convention countries a notice requesting the central authority of each such country to specify any requirements of such country regarding adoption, including restrictions on the eligibility of persons to adopt, with respect to which information on the prospective adoptive parent or parents in the United States would be relevant;

(3) making responses to notices under paragraph (2) available to—

(A) accredited agencies and approved persons; and

(B) other persons or entities performing home studies under section 201(b)(1);

(4) ensuring the provision of a background report (home study) on prospective adoptive parent or parents (pursuant to the requirements of section 203(b)(1)(A)(ii)), through the central authority of each child's country of origin, to the court having jurisdiction over the adoption (or, in the case of a child emigrating to the United States for the purpose of adoption, to the competent authority in the

child's country of origin with responsibility for approving the child's emigration) in adequate time to be considered prior to the granting of such adoption or approval;

(5) providing Federal agencies, State courts, and accredited agencies and approved persons with an identification of Convention countries and persons authorized to perform functions under the Convention in each such country; and

(6) facilitating the transmittal of other appropriate information to, and among, central authorities, Federal and State agencies (including State courts), and accredited agencies and approved persons.

(c) ACCREDITATION AND APPROVAL RESPONSIBILITIES—The Secretary shall carry out the functions prescribed by the Convention with respect to the accreditation of agencies and the approval of persons to provide adoption services in the United States in cases subject to the Convention as provided in title II. Such functions may not be delegated to any other Federal agency.

(d) ADDITIONAL RESPONSIBILITIES—The Secretary—

(1) shall monitor individual Convention adoption cases involving United States citizens; and

(2) may facilitate interactions between such citizens and officials of other Convention countries on matters relating to the Convention in any case in which an accredited agency or approved person is unwilling or unable to provide such facilitation.

(e) ESTABLISHMENT OF REGISTRY—The Secretary and the Attorney General shall jointly establish a case registry of all adoptions involving immigration of children into the United States and emigration of children from the United States, regardless of whether the adoption occurs under the Convention. Such registry shall permit tracking of pending cases and retrieval of information on both pending and closed cases.

(f) METHODS OF PERFORMING RESPONSIBILITIES—The Secretary may—

(1) authorize public or private entities to perform appropriate central authority functions for which the Secretary is responsible, pursuant to regulations or under agreements published in the Federal Register; and

(2) carry out central authority functions through grants to, or contracts with, any individual or public or private entity, except as may be otherwise specifically provided in this Act.

SEC. 103. RESPONSIBILITIES OF THE ATTORNEY GENERAL.

In addition to such other responsibilities as are specifically conferred upon the Attorney General by this Act, the central authority functions specified in Article 14 of the Convention (relating to the filing of applications by prospective adoptive parents to the central authority of their country of residence) shall be performed by the Attorney General.

SEC. 104. ANNUAL REPORT ON INTERCOUNTRY ADOPTIONS.

(a) REPORTS REQUIRED—Beginning 1 year after the date of the entry into force of the Convention for the United States and each year thereafter, the Secretary, in consultation with the Attorney General and other appropriate agencies, shall submit a report describing the activities of the central authority of the United States under this Act during the preceding year to the Committee on International Relations, the Committee on Ways and Means, and the Committee on the Judiciary of the House of Representatives and the Committee on Foreign Relations, the Committee on Finance, and the Committee on the Judiciary of the Senate.

(b) REPORT ELEMENTS—Each report under subsection (a) shall set forth with respect to the year concerned, the following:

(1) The number of intercountry adoptions involving immigration to the United States, regardless of whether the adoption occurred under the Convention, including the country from which each child emigrated, the State to which each child immigrated, and the country in which the adoption was finalized.

(2) The number of intercountry adoptions involving emigration from the United States, regardless of whether the adoption occurred under the Convention, including the country to which each child immigrated and the State from which each child emigrated.

(3) The number of Convention placements for adoption in the United States that were disrupted, including the country from which the child emigrated, the age of the child, the date of the placement for adoption, the reasons for the disruption, the resolution of the disruption, the agencies that handled the placement for adoption, and the plans for the child, and in addition, any information regarding disruption or dissolution of adoptions of children from other countries received pursuant to section 422(b)(14) of the Social Security Act, as amended by section 205 of this Act.

(4) The average time required for completion of a Convention adoption, set forth by country from which the child emigrated.

(5) The current list of agencies accredited and persons approved under this Act to provide adoption services.

(6) The names of the agencies and persons temporarily or permanently debarred under this Act, and the reasons for the debarment.

(7) The range of adoption fees charged in connection with Convention adoptions involving immigration to the United States and the median of such fees set forth by the country of origin.

(8) The range of fees charged for accreditation of agencies and the approval of persons in the United States engaged in providing adoption services under the Convention.

TITLE II—PROVISIONS RELATING TO ACCREDITATION AND APPROVAL

SEC. 201. ACCREDITATION OR APPROVAL REQUIRED IN ORDER TO PROVIDE ADOPTION SERVICES IN CASES SUBJECT TO THE CONVENTION.

(a) IN GENERAL—Except as otherwise provided in this title, no person may offer or provide adoption services in connection with a Convention adoption in the United States unless that person—

(1) is accredited or approved in accordance with this title; or

(2) is providing such services through or under the supervision and responsibility of an accredited agency or approved person.

(b) EXCEPTIONS—Subsection (a) shall not apply to the following:

(1) BACKGROUND STUDIES AND HOME STUDIES—The performance of a background study on a child or a home study on a prospective adoptive parent, or any report on any such study by a social work professional or organization who is not providing any other adoption service in the case, if the background or home study is approved by an accredited agency.

(2) CHILD WELFARE SERVICES—The provision of a child welfare service by a person who is not providing any other adoption service in the case.

(3) LEGAL SERVICES—The provision of legal services by a person who is not providing any adoption service in the case.

(4) PROSPECTIVE ADOPTIVE PARENTS ACTING ON OWN BEHALF—The conduct of a prospective adoptive parent on his or her

own behalf in the case, to the extent not prohibited by the law of the State in which the prospective adoptive parent resides.

SEC. 202. PROCESS FOR ACCREDITATION AND APPROVAL; ROLE OF ACCREDITING ENTITIES.

(a) DESIGNATION OF ACCREDITING ENTITIES—

(1) IN GENERAL—The Secretary shall enter into agreements with one or more qualified entities under which such entities will perform the duties described in subsection (b) in accordance with the Convention, this title, and the regulations prescribed under section 203, and upon entering into each such agreement shall designate the qualified entity as an accrediting entity.

(2) QUALIFIED ENTITIES—In paragraph (1), the term "qualified entity" means—

(A) a nonprofit private entity that has expertise in developing and administering standards for entities providing child welfare services and that meets such other criteria as the Secretary may by regulation establish; or

(B) a public entity (other than a Federal entity), including an agency or instrumentality of State government having responsibility for licensing adoption agencies, that—

(i) has expertise in developing and administering standards for entities providing child welfare services;

(ii) accredits only agencies located in the State in which the public entity is located; and

(iii) meets such other criteria as the Secretary may by regulation establish.

(b) DUTIES OF ACCREDITING ENTITIES—The duties described in this subsection are the following:

(1) ACCREDITATION AND APPROVAL—Accreditation of agencies, and approval of persons, to provide adoption services in the United States in cases subject to the Convention.

(2) OVERSIGHT—Ongoing monitoring of the compliance of accredited agencies and approved persons with applicable requirements, including review of complaints against such agencies and persons in accordance with procedures established by the accrediting entity and approved by the Secretary.

(3) ENFORCEMENT—Taking of adverse actions (including requiring corrective action, imposing sanctions, and refusing to renew, suspending, or canceling accreditation or approval) for noncompliance with applicable requirements, and notifying the agency or person against whom adverse actions are taken of the deficiencies necessitating the adverse action.

(4) DATA, RECORDS, AND REPORTS—Collection of data, maintenance of records, and reporting to the Secretary, the United States central authority, State courts, and other entities (including on persons and agencies granted or denied approval or accreditation), to the extent and in the manner that the Secretary requires.

(c) REMEDIES FOR ADVERSE ACTION BY ACCREDITING ENTITY—

(1) CORRECTION OF DEFICIENCY—An agency or person who is the subject of an adverse action by an accrediting entity may re-apply for accreditation or approval (or petition for termination of the adverse action) on demonstrating to the satisfaction of the accrediting entity that the deficiencies necessitating the adverse action have been corrected.

(2) NO OTHER ADMINISTRATIVE REVIEW—An adverse action by an accrediting entity shall not be subject to administrative review.

(3) JUDICIAL REVIEW—An agency or person who is the subject of an adverse action by an accrediting entity may petition the United States district court in the judicial district in which the agency is located or the person resides to set aside the adverse action. The court shall review the adverse action in accordance with section 706 of title 5, United States Code, and for purposes of such review the accrediting entity shall be considered an agency within the meaning of section 701 of such title.

(d) FEES—The amount of fees assessed by accrediting entities for the costs of accreditation shall be subject to approval by the Secretary. Such fees may not exceed the costs of accreditation. In reviewing the level of such fees, the Secretary shall consider the relative size of, the geographic location of, and the number of Convention adoption cases managed by the agencies or persons subject to accreditation or approval by the accrediting entity.

SEC. 203. STANDARDS AND PROCEDURES FOR PROVIDING ACCREDITATION OR APPROVAL.

(a) IN GENERAL—

(1) PROMULGATION OF REGULATIONS—The Secretary, shall, by regulation, prescribe the standards and procedures to be used by accrediting entities for the accreditation of agencies and the approval of persons to provide adoption services in the United States in cases subject to the Convention.

(2) CONSIDERATION OF VIEWS—In developing such regulations, the Secretary shall consider any standards or procedures developed or proposed by, and the views of, individuals and entities with interest and expertise in international adoptions and family social services, including public and private entities with experience in licensing and accrediting adoption agencies.

(3) APPLICABILITY OF NOTICE AND COMMENT RULES—Subsections (b), (c), and (d) of section 553 of title 5, United States Code, shall apply in the development and issuance of regulations under this section.

(b) MINIMUM REQUIREMENTS—

(1) ACCREDITATION—The standards prescribed under subsection (a) shall include the requirement that accreditation of an agency may not be provided or continued under this title unless the agency meets the following requirements:

(A) SPECIFIC REQUIREMENTS—

(i) The agency provides prospective adoptive parents of a child in a prospective Convention adoption a copy of the medical records of the child (which, to the fullest extent practicable, shall include an English-language translation of such records) on a date which is not later than the earlier of the date that is 2 weeks before: (I) the adoption; or (II) the date on which the prospective parents travel to a foreign country to complete all procedures in such country relating to the adoption.

(ii) The agency ensures that a thorough background report (home study) on the prospective adoptive parent or parents has been completed in accordance with the Convention and with applicable Federal and State requirements and transmitted to the Attorney General with respect to each Convention adoption. Each such report shall include a criminal background check and a full and complete statement of all facts relevant to the eligibility of the prospective adopting parent or parents to adopt a child under any requirements specified by the central authority of the child's country of origin under section 102(b)(3), including, in the case of a child emigrating to the United States for the purpose of adoption, the requirements of the child's country of origin applicable to adoptions taking place in such country. For purposes of this clause, the term "background report (home study)" includes any supplemental statement submitted by the agency to the Attorney General for the purpose of providing information relevant to any requirements specified by the child's country of origin.

(iii) The agency provides prospective adoptive parents with a training program that includes counseling and guidance for the purpose of promoting a successful intercountry adoption before such parents travel to adopt the child or the child is placed with such parents for adoption.

(iv) The agency employs personnel providing intercountry adoption services on a fee for service basis rather than on a contingent fee basis.

(v) The agency discloses fully its policies and practices, the disruption rates of its placements for intercountry adoption, and all fees charged by such agency for intercountry adoption.

(B) CAPACITY TO PROVIDE ADOPTION SERVICES—The agency has, directly or through arrangements with other persons, a sufficient number of appropriately trained and qualified personnel, sufficient financial resources, appropriate organizational structure, and appropriate procedures to enable the agency to provide, in accordance with this Act, all adoption services in cases subject to the Convention.

(C) USE OF SOCIAL SERVICE PROFESSIONALS—The agency has established procedures designed to ensure that social service functions requiring the application of clinical skills and judgment are performed only by professionals with appropriate qualifications and credentials.

(D) RECORDS, REPORTS, AND INFORMATION MATTERS—The agency is capable of—

(i) maintaining such records and making such reports as may be required by the Secretary, the United States central authority, and the accrediting entity that accredits the agency;

(ii) cooperating with reviews, inspections, and audits;

(iii) safeguarding sensitive individual information; and

(iv) complying with other requirements concerning information management necessary to ensure compliance with the Convention, this Act, and any other applicable law.

(E) LIABILITY INSURANCE—The agency agrees to have in force adequate liability insurance for professional negligence and any other insurance that the Secretary considers appropriate.

(F) COMPLIANCE WITH APPLICABLE RULES—The agency has established adequate measures to comply (and to ensure compliance of their agents and clients) with the Convention, this Act, and any other applicable law.

(G) NONPROFIT ORGANIZATION WITH STATE LICENSE TO PROVIDE ADOPTION SERVICES—The agency is a private nonprofit organization licensed to provide adoption services in at least one State.

(2) APPROVAL—The standards prescribed under subsection (a) shall include the requirement that a person shall not be approved under this title unless the person is a private for-profit entity that meets the requirements of subparagraphs (A) through (F) of paragraph (1) of this subsection.

(3) RENEWAL OF ACCREDITATION OR APPROVAL—The standards prescribed under subsection (a) shall provide that the accreditation of an agency or approval of a person under this title shall be for a period of not less than 3 years and not more than 5 years, and may be renewed on a showing that the agency or person meets the requirements applicable to original accreditation or approval under this title.

(c) TEMPORARY REGISTRATION OF COMMUNITY BASED AGENCIES—

(1) ONE-YEAR REGISTRATION PERIOD FOR MEDIUM COMMUNITY BASED AGENCIES—For a 1-year period after the entry into force of the Convention and notwithstanding subsection (b), the Secretary may provide, in regulations issued pursuant to subsection (a), that an agency may register with the Secretary and be accredited to provide adoption services in the United States in cases subject to the Convention during such period if the agency has provided adoption services in fewer than 100 intercountry adoptions in the preceding calendar year and meets the criteria described in paragraph (3).

(2) TWO-YEAR REGISTRATION PERIOD FOR SMALL COMMUNITY-BASED AGENCIES—For a 2-year period after the entry into force of the Convention and notwithstanding subsection (b), the Sec-

retary may provide, in regulations issued pursuant to subsection (a), that an agency may register with the Secretary and be accredited to provide adoption services in the United States in cases subject to the Convention during such period if the agency has provided adoption services in fewer than 50 intercountry adoptions in the preceding calendar year and meets the criteria described in paragraph (3).

(3) CRITERIA FOR REGISTRATION—Agencies registered under this subsection shall meet the following criteria:

(A) The agency is licensed in the State in which it is located and is a nonprofit agency.

(B) The agency has been providing adoption services in connection with intercountry adoptions for at least 3 years.

(C) The agency has demonstrated that it will be able to provide the United States Government with all information related to the elements described in section 104(b) and provides such information.

(D) The agency has initiated the process of becoming accredited under the provisions of this Act and is actively taking steps to become an accredited agency.

(E) The agency has not been found to be involved in any improper conduct relating to intercountry adoptions.

SEC. 204. SECRETARIAL OVERSIGHT OF ACCREDITATION AND APPROVAL.

(a) OVERSIGHT OF ACCREDITING ENTITIES—The Secretary shall—

(1) monitor the performance by each accrediting entity of its duties under section 202 and its compliance with the requirements of the Convention, this Act, other applicable laws, and implementing regulations under this Act; and

(2) suspend or cancel the designation of an accrediting entity found to be substantially out of compliance with the Convention, this Act, other applicable laws, or implementing regulations under this Act.

(b) SUSPENSION OR CANCELLATION OF ACCREDITATION OR APPROVAL—

(1) SECRETARY'S AUTHORITY—The Secretary shall suspend or cancel the accreditation or approval granted by an accrediting entity to

an agency or person pursuant to section 202 when the Secretary finds that—

(A) the agency or person is substantially out of compliance with applicable requirements; and

(B) the accrediting entity has failed or refused, after consultation with the Secretary, to take appropriate enforcement action.

(2) CORRECTION OF DEFICIENCY—At any time when the Secretary is satisfied that the deficiencies on the basis of which an adverse action is taken under paragraph (1) have been corrected, the Secretary shall—

(A) notify the accrediting entity that the deficiencies have been corrected; and

(B)(i) in the case of a suspension, terminate the suspension; or

(ii) in the case of a cancellation, notify the agency or person that the agency or person may re-apply to the accrediting entity for accreditation or approval.

(c) DEBARMENT—

(1) SECRETARY'S AUTHORITY—On the initiative of the Secretary, or on request of an accrediting entity, the Secretary may temporarily or permanently debar an agency from accreditation or a person from approval under this title, but only if—

(A) there is substantial evidence that the agency or person is out of compliance with applicable requirements; and

(B) there has been a pattern of serious, willful, or grossly negligent failures to comply or other aggravating circumstances indicating that continued accreditation or approval would not be in the best interests of the children and families concerned.

(2) PERIOD OF DEBARMENT—The Secretary's debarment order shall state whether the debarment is temporary or permanent. If the debarment is temporary, the Secretary shall specify a date, not earlier than 3 years after the date of the order, on or after which the agency or person may apply to the Secretary for withdrawal of the debarment.

(3) EFFECT OF DEBARMENT—An accrediting entity may take into account the circumstances of the debarment of an agency or person that has been debarred pursuant to this subsection in considering any subsequent application of the agency or person, or of any other

entity in which the agency or person has an ownership or control interest, for accreditation or approval under this title.

(d) JUDICIAL REVIEW—A person (other than a prospective adoptive parent), an agency, or an accrediting entity who is the subject of a final action of suspension, cancellation, or debarment by the Secretary under this title may petition the United States District Court for the District of Columbia or the United States district court in the judicial district in which the person resides or the agency or accrediting entity is located to set aside the action. The court shall review the action in accordance with section 706 of title 5, United States Code.

(e) FAILURE TO ENSURE A FULL AND COMPLETE HOME STUDY—

(1) IN GENERAL—Willful, grossly negligent, or repeated failure to ensure the completion and transmission of a background report (home study) that fully complies with the requirements of section 203(b)(1)(A)(ii) shall constitute substantial noncompliance with applicable requirements.

(2) REGULATIONS—Regulations promulgated under section 203 shall provide for—

(A) frequent and careful monitoring of compliance by agencies and approved persons with the requirements of section 203(b)(A)(ii); and

(B) consultation between the Secretary and the accrediting entity where an agency or person has engaged in substantial noncompliance with the requirements of section 203(b)(A)(ii), unless the accrediting entity has taken appropriate corrective action and the noncompliance has not recurred.

(3) REPEATED FAILURES TO COMPLY—Repeated serious, willful, or grossly negligent failures to comply with the requirements of section 203(b)(1)(A)(ii) by an agency or person after consultation between Secretary and the accrediting entity with respect to previous noncompliance by such agency or person shall constitute a pattern of serious, willful, or grossly negligent failures to comply under subsection (c)(1)(B).

(4) FAILURE TO COMPLY WITH CERTAIN REQUIREMENTS—A failure to comply with the requirements of section 203(b)(1)(A)(ii) shall constitute a serious failure to comply under subsection (c)(1)(B) unless it is shown by clear and convincing evidence that such noncompliance had neither the purpose nor the effect of determining the outcome of a decision or proceeding by a court or other competent authority in the United States or the child's country of origin.

SEC. 205. STATE PLAN REQUIREMENT.

Section 422(b) of the Social Security Act (42 U.S.C. 622(b)) is amended—

(1) in paragraph (11), by striking "and" at the end;

(2) in paragraph (12), by striking "children," and inserting "children;"; and

(3) by adding at the end the following new paragraphs:

"(13) contain a description of the activities that the State has undertaken for children adopted from other countries, including the provision of adoption and post-adoption services; and

"(14) provide that the State shall collect and report information on children who are adopted from other countries and who enter into State custody as a result of the disruption of a placement for adoption or the dissolution of an adoption, including the number of children, the agencies who handled the placement or adoption, the plans for the child, and the reasons for the disruption or dissolution.".

TITLE III—RECOGNITION OF CONVENTION ADOPTIONS IN THE UNITED STATES

SEC. 301. ADOPTIONS OF CHILDREN IMMIGRATING TO THE UNITED STATES.

(a) LEGAL EFFECT OF CERTIFICATES ISSUED BY THE SECRETARY OF STATE—

(1) ISSUANCE OF CERTIFICATES BY THE SECRETARY OF STATE—The Secretary of State shall, with respect to each Convention adoption, issue a certificate to the adoptive citizen parent domiciled in the United States that the adoption has been granted or, in the case of a prospective adoptive citizen parent, that legal custody of the child has been granted to the citizen parent for purposes of emigration and adoption, pursuant to the Convention and this Act, if the Secretary of State—

(A) receives appropriate notification from the central authority of such child's country of origin; and

(B) has verified that the requirements of the Convention and this Act have been met with respect to the adoption.

(2) LEGAL EFFECT OF CERTIFICATES—If appended to an original adoption decree, the certificate described in paragraph (1) shall be treated by Federal and State agencies, courts, and other public and

private persons and entities as conclusive evidence of the facts certified therein and shall constitute the certification required by section 204(d)(2) of the Immigration and Nationality Act, as amended by this Act.

(b) LEGAL EFFECT OF CONVENTION ADOPTION FINALIZED IN ANOTHER CONVENTION COUNTRY—A final adoption in another Convention country, certified by the Secretary of State pursuant to subsection (a) of this section or section 303(c), shall be recognized as a final valid adoption for purposes of all Federal, State, and local laws of the United States.

(c) CONDITION ON FINALIZATION OF CONVENTION ADOPTION BY STATE COURT—In the case of a child who has entered the United States from another Convention country for the purpose of adoption, an order declaring the adoption final shall not be entered unless the Secretary of State has issued the certificate provided for in subsection (a) with respect to the adoption.

SEC. 302. IMMIGRATION AND NATIONALITY ACT AMENDMENTS RELATING TO CHILDREN ADOPTED FROM CONVENTION COUNTRIES.

(a) DEFINITION OF CHILD—Section 101(b)(1) of the Immigration and Nationality Act (8 U.S.C. 1101(b)(1)) is amended—

(1) by striking "or" at the end of subparagraph (E);

(2) by striking the period at the end of subparagraph (F) and inserting "; or"; and

(3) by adding after subparagraph (F) the following new subparagraph:

"(G) a child, under the age of sixteen at the time a petition is filed on the child's behalf to accord a classification as an immediate relative under section 201(b), who has been adopted in a foreign state that is a party to the Convention on Protection of Children and Co-operation in Respect of Intercountry Adoption done at The Hague on May 29, 1993, or who is emigrating from such a foreign state to be adopted in the United States, by a United States citizen and spouse jointly, or by an unmarried United States citizen at least 25 years of age—

"(i) if—

"(I) the Attorney General is satisfied that proper care will be furnished the child if admitted to the United States;

"(II) the child's natural parents (or parent, in the case of a child who has one sole or surviving parent because of the death or disappearance of, abandonment or desertion by, the other parent), or other persons or institutions that retain legal custody of the child, have freely given their written irrevocable consent to the termination of their legal relationship with the child, and to the child's emigration and adoption;

"(III) in the case of a child having two living natural parents, the natural parents are incapable of providing proper care for the child;

"(IV) the Attorney General is satisfied that the purpose of the adoption is to form a bona fide parent-child relationship, and the parent-child relationship of the child and the natural parents has been terminated (and in carrying out both obligations under this subclause the Attorney General may consider whether there is a petition pending to confer immigrant status on one or both of such natural parents); and

"(V) in the case of a child who has not been adopted—

"(aa) the competent authority of the foreign state has approved the child's emigration to the United States for the purpose of adoption by the prospective adoptive parent or parents; and

"(bb) the prospective adoptive parent or parents has or have complied with any pre-adoption requirements of the child's proposed residence; and

"(ii) except that no natural parent or prior adoptive parent of any such child shall thereafter, by virtue of such parentage, be accorded any right, privilege, or status under this Act.".

(b) APPROVAL OF PETITIONS—Section 204(d) of the Immigration and Nationality Act (8 U.S.C. 1154(d)) is amended—

(1) by striking "(d)" and inserting "(d)(1)";

(2) by striking "section 101(b)(1)(F)" and inserting "subparagraph (F) or (G) of section 101(b)(1)"; and

(3) by adding at the end the following new paragraph:

"(2) Notwithstanding the provisions of subsections (a) and (b), no petition may be approved on behalf of a child defined in section 101(b)(1)(G) unless the Secretary of State has certified that the central authority of the child's country of origin has notified the United States central authority under the convention referred to in such section 101(b)(1)(G) that a United States citizen habitually resident in the United States has effected final adoption of the child, or has been granted custody of the child for the purpose of emigration and adoption, in accordance with such convention and the Intercountry Adoption Act of 2000.".

(c) DEFINITION OF PARENT—Section 101(b)(2) of the Immigration and Nationality Act (8 U.S.C. 1101(b)(2)) is amended by inserting "and paragraph (1)(G)(i)" after "second proviso therein)".

SEC. 303. ADOPTIONS OF CHILDREN EMIGRATING FROM THE UNITED STATES.

(a) DUTIES OF ACCREDITED AGENCY OR APPROVED PERSON—In the case of a Convention adoption involving the emigration of a child residing in the United States to a foreign country, the accredited agency or approved person providing adoption services, or the prospective adoptive parent or parents acting on their own behalf (if permitted by the laws of such other Convention country in which they reside and the laws of the State in which the child resides), shall do the following:

(1) Ensure that, in accordance with the Convention—

(A) a background study on the child is completed;

(B) the accredited agency or approved person—

(i) has made reasonable efforts to actively recruit and make a diligent search for prospective adoptive parents to adopt the child in the United States; and

(ii) despite such efforts, has not been able to place the child for adoption in the United States in a timely manner; and

(C) a determination is made that placement with the prospective adoptive parent or parents is in the best interests of the child.

(2) Furnish to the State court with jurisdiction over the case—

(A) documentation of the matters described in paragraph (1);

(B) a background report (home study) on the prospective adoptive parent or parents (including a criminal background check) prepared in accordance with the laws of the receiving country; and

(C) a declaration by the central authority (or other competent authority) of such other Convention country—

(i) that the child will be permitted to enter and reside permanently, or on the same basis as the adopting parent, in the receiving country; and

(ii) that the central authority (or other competent authority) of such other Convention country consents to the adoption, if such consent is necessary under the laws of such country for the adoption to become final.

(3) Furnish to the United States central authority—

(A) official copies of State court orders certifying the final adoption or grant of custody for the purpose of adoption;

(B) the information and documents described in paragraph (2), to the extent required by the United States central authority; and

(C) any other information concerning the case required by the United States central authority to perform the functions specified in subsection (c) or otherwise to carry out the duties of the United States central authority under the Convention.

(b) CONDITIONS ON STATE COURT ORDERS—An order declaring an adoption to be final or granting custody for the purpose of adoption in a case described in subsection (a) shall not be entered unless the court—

(1) has received and verified to the extent the court may find necessary—

(A) the material described in subsection (a)(2); and

(B) satisfactory evidence that the requirements of Articles 4 and 15 through 21 of the Convention have been met; and

(2) has determined that the adoptive placement is in the best interests of the child.

(c) DUTIES OF THE SECRETARY OF STATE—In a case described in subsection (a), the Secretary, on receipt and verification as necessary of the material and information described in subsection (a)(3), shall issue, as applicable, an official certification that the child has been adopted or a declaration that custody for purposes of adoption has been granted, in accordance with the Convention and this Act.

(d) FILING WITH REGISTRY REGARDING NONCONVENTION ADOPTIONS—Accredited agencies, approved persons, and other persons, including governmental authorities, providing adoption services in an intercountry adoption not subject to the Convention that involves the emigration of a child from the United States shall file information required by regulations jointly issued by the Attorney General and the Secretary of State for purposes of implementing section 102(e).

TITLE IV—ADMINISTRATION AND ENFORCEMENT

SEC. 401. ACCESS TO CONVENTION RECORDS.

(a) PRESERVATION OF CONVENTION RECORDS—

(1) IN GENERAL—Not later than 180 days after the date of the enactment of this Act, the Secretary, in consultation with the Attorney General, shall issue regulations that establish procedures and requirements in accordance with the Convention and this section for the preservation of Convention records.

(2) APPLICABILITY OF NOTICE AND COMMENT RULES—Subsections (b), (c), and (d) of section 553 of title 5, United States Code, shall apply in the development and issuance of regulations under this section.

(b) ACCESS TO CONVENTION RECORDS—

(1) PROHIBITION—Except as provided in paragraph (2), the Secretary or the Attorney General may disclose a Convention record, and access to such a record may be provided in whole or in part, only if such record is maintained under the authority of the Immigration and Nationality Act and disclosure of, or access to, such record is permitted or required by applicable Federal law.

(2) EXCEPTION FOR ADMINISTRATION OF THE CONVENTION—A Convention record may be disclosed, and access to such a record may be provided, in whole or in part, among the Secretary, the Attorney General, central authorities, accredited agencies, and approved persons, only to the extent necessary to administer the Convention or this Act.

(3) PENALTIES FOR UNLAWFUL DISCLOSURE—Unlawful disclosure of all or part of a Convention record shall be punishable in accordance with applicable Federal law.

(c) ACCESS TO NON-CONVENTION RECORDS—Disclosure of, access to, and penalties for unlawful disclosure of, adoption records that are not Convention records, including records of adoption proceedings conducted in the United States, shall be governed by applicable State law.

SEC. 402. DOCUMENTS OF OTHER CONVENTION COUNTRIES.

Documents originating in any other Convention country and related to a Convention adoption case shall require no authentication in order to be admissible in any Federal, State, or local court in the United States, unless a specific and supported claim is made that the documents are false, have been altered, or are otherwise unreliable.

SEC. 403. AUTHORIZATION OF APPROPRIATIONS; COLLECTION OF FEES.

(a) AUTHORIZATION OF APPROPRIATIONS—

(1) IN GENERAL—There are authorized to be appropriated such sums as may be necessary to agencies of the Federal Government implementing the Convention and the provisions of this Act.

(2) AVAILABILITY OF FUNDS—Amounts appropriated pursuant to paragraph (1) are authorized to remain available until expended.

(b) ASSESSMENT OF FEES—

(1) The Secretary may charge a fee for new or enhanced services that will be undertaken by the Department of State to meet the requirements of this Act with respect to intercountry adoptions under the Convention and comparable services with respect to other intercountry adoptions. Such fee shall be prescribed by regulation and shall not exceed the cost of such services.

(2) Fees collected under paragraph (1) shall be retained and deposited as an offsetting collection to any Department of State appropriation to recover the costs of providing such services.

(3) Fees authorized under this section shall be available for obligation only to the extent and in the amount provided in advance in appropriations Acts.

(c) RESTRICTION—No funds collected under the authority of this section may be made available to an accrediting entity to carry out the purposes of this Act.

SEC. 404. ENFORCEMENT.

(a) CIVIL PENALTIES—Any person who—

(1) violates section 201;

(2) makes a false or fraudulent statement, or misrepresentation, with respect to a material fact, or offers, gives, solicits, or accepts inducement by way of compensation, intended to influence or affect in the United States or a foreign country—

(A) a decision by an accrediting entity with respect to the accreditation of an agency or approval of a person under title II;

(B) the relinquishment of parental rights or the giving of parental consent relating to the adoption of a child in a case subject to the Convention; or

(C) a decision or action of any entity performing a central authority function; or

(3) engages another person as an agent, whether in the United States or in a foreign country, who in the course of that agency takes any of the actions described in paragraph (1) or (2), shall be subject, in addition to any other penalty that may be prescribed by law, to a civil money penalty of not more than $50,000 for a first violation, and not more than $100,000 for each succeeding violation.

(b) CIVIL ENFORCEMENT—

(1) AUTHORITY OF ATTORNEY GENERAL—The Attorney General may bring a civil action to enforce subsection (a) against any person in any United States district court.

(2) FACTORS TO BE CONSIDERED IN IMPOSING PENALTIES—In imposing penalties the court shall consider the gravity of the violation, the degree of culpability of the defendant, and any history of prior violations by the defendant.

(c) CRIMINAL PENALTIES—Whoever knowingly and willfully violates paragraph (1) or (2) of subsection (a) shall be subject to a fine of not more than $250,000, imprisonment for not more than 5 years, or both.

TITLE V—GENERAL PROVISIONS

SEC. 501. RECOGNITION OF CONVENTION ADOPTIONS.

Subject to Article 24 of the Convention, adoptions concluded between two other Convention countries that meet the requirements of Article 23 of the Convention and that became final before the date of entry into force of the Convention for the United States shall be recognized thereafter in the United States and given full effect. Such recognition shall include the specific effects described in Article 26 of the Convention.

SEC. 502. SPECIAL RULES FOR CERTAIN CASES.

(a) AUTHORITY TO ESTABLISH ALTERNATIVE PROCEDURES FOR ADOPTION OF CHILDREN BY RELATIVES—To the extent consistent with the Convention, the Secretary may establish by regulation alternative procedures for the adoption of children by individuals related to them by blood, marriage, or adoption, in cases subject to the Convention.

(b) WAIVER AUTHORITY—

(1) IN GENERAL—Notwithstanding any other provision of this Act, to the extent consistent with the Convention, the Secretary may, on a case-by-case basis, waive applicable requirements of this Act or regulations issued under this Act, in the interests of justice or to prevent grave physical harm to the child.

(2) NONDELEGATION—The authority provided by paragraph (1) may not be delegated.

SEC. 503. RELATIONSHIP TO OTHER LAWS.

(a) PREEMPTION OF INCONSISTENT STATE LAW—The Convention and this Act shall not be construed to preempt any provision of the law of any State or political subdivision thereof, or prevent a State or political subdivision thereof from enacting any provision of law with respect to the subject matter of the Convention or this Act, except to the extent that such provision of State law is inconsistent with the Convention or this Act, and then only to the extent of the inconsistency.

(b) APPLICABILITY OF THE INDIAN CHILD WELFARE ACT—The Convention and this Act shall not be construed to affect the application of the Indian Child Welfare Act of 1978 (25 U.S.C. 1901 et seq.).

(c) RELATIONSHIP TO OTHER LAWS—Sections 3506(c), 3507, and 3512 of title 44, United States Code, shall not apply to information collection for purposes of sections 104, 202(b)(4), and 303(d) of this Act or for use as a Convention record as defined in this Act.

SEC. 504. NO PRIVATE RIGHT OF ACTION.

The Convention and this Act shall not be construed to create a private right of action to seek administrative or judicial relief, except to the extent expressly provided in this Act.

SEC. 505. EFFECTIVE DATES; TRANSITION RULE.

(a) EFFECTIVE DATES—

(1) PROVISIONS EFFECTIVE UPON ENACTMENT—Sections 2, 3, 101 through 103, 202 through 205, 401(a), 403, 503, and 505(a) shall take effect on the date of the enactment of this Act.

(2) PROVISIONS EFFECTIVE UPON THE ENTRY INTO FORCE OF THE CONVENTION—Subject to subsection (b), the provisions of this Act not specified in paragraph (1) shall take effect upon the entry into force of the Convention for the United States pursuant to Article 46(2)(a) of the Convention.

(b) TRANSITION RULE—The Convention and this Act shall not apply—

(1) in the case of a child immigrating to the United States, if the application for advance processing of an orphan petition or petition to classify an orphan as an immediate relative for the child is filed before the effective date described in subsection (a)(2); or

(2) in the case of a child emigrating from the United States, if the prospective adoptive parents of the child initiated the adoption process in their country of residence with the filing of an appropriate application before the effective date described in subsection (a)(2).

APPENDIX 13:
DIRECTORY OF NATIONAL ADOPTION ORGANIZATIONS AND PARENT SUPPORT GROUPS

NAME	ADDRESS	TELEPHONE	FAX	WEBSITE	E-MAIL
National Adoption Information Clearinghouse (NAIC)	P.O. Box 1182 Washington, DC 20013-1182	703-352-3488	703-385-3206	http://www.calib.com/naic	Naic@calib.com
Adoptive Families Magazine	P.O. Box 5159 Brentwood, TN 37024	1-800-372-3300	N/A	http://www.adoptivefamilies magazine.com	N/A
Committee for Single Adoptive Parents, Inc.	P.O. Box 15084 Chevy Chase, MD 20825	202-966-6367	N/A	N/A	N/A
FACE (Families Adopting Children Everywhere) Face Inc.	P.O. Box 28058 Baltimore, MD 21239	410-488-2656	N/A	http://www.face2000.org	N/A

NAME	ADDRESS	TELEPHONE	FAX	WEBSITE	E-MAIL
International Concerns Committee for Children	911 Cypress Drive Boulder, CO 80303	303-494-8333	N/A	http://www.iccadopt.org	N/A
Joint Council on International Children's Services	1320 19th St. NW Suite 200 Washington, DC 20036	202-429-0400	N/A	http://www.jcics.org	N/A
North American Council on Adoptable Children (NACAC)	970 Raymond Avenue Suite 106 St. Paul, MN 55114	651-644-3036	651-644-9848	http://www.nacac.org	N/A
National Council for Adoption	1930 17th Street, NW Washington, DC 20009	202-328-1200	N/A	http://www.ncfa-usa.org	N/A

APPENDIX 14:
SECTIONS OF LAW AND REGULATION
RELATING TO ORPHAN PETITIONS

THE IMMIGRATION AND NATIONALITY ACT (INA)

SECTION OF LAW	SUBJECT MATTER
Section 101(b)(1)(E) [8 U.S. Code (U.S.C.) 1101(b)(1)(E)]	Adopted children (other than orphans)
Section 101(b)(1)(F) [8 U.S.C. 1101(b)(1)(F)]	Orphans
Section 204(a), (b), (c) and (d) [8 U.S.C. 1154(a), (b), (c) and (d)]	Procedures for granting immigrant status
Section 205 (8 U.S.C. 1155)	Revocation of approval of petitions; notice of revocations; effective date

THE CODE OF FEDERAL REGULATIONS (CFR)

SECTION OF REGULATIONS	SUBJECT MATTER
Title 8, CFR 204.2	Petitions for relatives, widows and widowers, and abused spouses and children
Title 8, CFR 204.3	Orphans
Title 8, CFR 205	Revocation

GLOSSARY

Abandonment by Parents—Refers to a situation where the child's parents have willfully forsaken all parental rights, obligations and claims to the child, as well as all control over and possession of the child, without intending to transfer, or without transferring, these rights to any specific person(s). Abandonment must include not only the intention to surrender all parental rights, obligations and claims to the child, and control over and possession of the child, but also the actual act of surrendering such rights, obligations, claims, control and possession.

Acknowledgement—A formal declaration of one's signature before a notary public.

Adopted Child—Under the Immigration and Nationality Act, an adopted child is defined as a child adopted while under the age of sixteen years who has been in the legal custody of, and has resided with, the adopting parent or parents for at least two years, provided that no natural parent of any such adopted child shall thereafter, by virtue of such parentage, be accorded any right, privilege, or status. A child who is a natural sibling of an adopted child described above, and who was adopted by the adoptive parent or parents of the sibling while the child was under the age of eighteen, is also a child as under the Act.

Adult member of Prospective Adoptive Parents' Household—Refers to an individual, other than the prospective adoptive parent, over the age of 18, whose principal or only residence is the home of the prospective adoptive parents.

Advance Processing Application—Refers to the completion and submission of an Application for Advance Processing of Orphan Petition (Form I-600A), in accordance with the form's instructions, along with the required supporting documentation and fee, which must be signed by the married petitioner and spouse, or by the unmarried petitioner.

Affidavit—A sworn or affirmed statement made in writing and signed; if sworn, it is notarized.

American Bar Association (ABA)—A national organization of lawyers and law students.

Attestation—The act of witnessing an instrument in writing at the request of the party making the same, and subscribing it as a witness.

Competent Authority—A court or governmental agency of a foreign-sending country having jurisdiction and authority to make decisions in matters of child welfare, including adoption.

Constitution—The fundamental principles of law which frame a governmental system.

Constitutional Right—Refers to the individual liberties granted by the constitution of a state or the federal government.

Co-residency—Evidence that the adoptive parent and child reside together in a familial relationship under which the adoptive parent asserts parental control, e.g. provides financial support, supervision, living arrangement in adoptive parent's home, etc.

Decree—A decision or order of the court.

Desertion by Parents—Refers to a situation where the parents have willfully forsaken their child and have refused to carry out their parental rights and obligations and that, as a result, the child has become a ward of a competent authority in accordance with the laws of the foreign-sending country.

Disappearance of Parents—Refers to a situation where both parents have unaccountably or inexplicably passed out of the child's life, their whereabouts are unknown, there is no reasonable hope of their reappearance and there has been a reasonable effort to locate them as determined by a competent authority in accordance with the laws of the foreign-sending country.

Due Process Rights—All rights which are of such fundamental importance as to require compliance with due process standards of fairness and justice.

Foreign-sending Country—The country of the orphan's citizenship, or if he or she is not permanently residing in the country of citizenship, the country of the orphan's habitual residence. This excludes a country to which the orphan travels temporarily, or to which he or she travels either as a prelude to, or in conjunction with, his or her adoption and/or immigration to the United States.

Fraud—A false representation of a matter of fact, whether by words or by conduct, by false or misleading allegations, or by concealment of that which should have been disclosed, which deceives and is intended to deceive another, and thereby causes injury to that person.

Home Study Preparer—Any party licensed or otherwise authorized under the law of the state of the orphan's proposed residence to conduct the research and preparation for a home study, including the required personal interview(s). This term includes a public agency with authority under that state's law in adoption matters, public or private adoption agencies licensed or otherwise authorized by the laws of that state to place children for adoption, and organizations or individuals licensed or otherwise authorized to conduct the research and preparation for a home study, under the laws of the state of the orphan's proposed residence. In the case of an orphan whose adoption has been finalized abroad and whose adoptive parents reside abroad, the home study preparer includes any party licensed or otherwise authorized to conduct home studies under the law of any state of the United States, or any party licensed or otherwise authorized by the foreign country's adoption authorities to conduct home studies under the laws of the foreign country.

Incapable of Providing Proper Care—Refers to a situation where the sole or surviving parent is unable to provide for the child's basic needs, consistent with the local standards of the foreign-sending country.

Legal Aid—A national organization established to provide legal services to those who are unable to afford private representation.

Legal Custody—The assumption of responsibility for a minor by an adult under the laws of the state and under the order or approval of a court of law or other appropriate government entity.

Loss from Both Parents—Refers to the involuntary severance or detachment of the child from the parents in a permanent manner such as that caused by a natural disaster, civil unrest or other calamitous event beyond the control of the parents, as verified by a competent authority in accordance with the laws of the foreign-sending country.

Orphan—Under the Immigration and Nationality Act, an orphan is defined as a child, under the age of sixteen at the time a petition is filed in his behalf to accord a classification as an immediate relative under the Act, who is an orphan because of the death or disappearance of, abandonment or desertion by, or separation or loss from both parents, or for whom the sole or surviving parent is incapable of providing the proper care and has in writing irrevocably released the child for emigration and adoption; who has been adopted abroad by a U.S. citizen and spouse jointly, or by an unmarried U.S. citizen at least twenty-five years of age, who personally saw and observed the child prior to or during the adoption proceedings; or who is coming to the United States for adoption by a U.S. citizen and spouse jointly, or by an unmarried U.S. citizen at least twenty-five years of age, who have or has complied with the preadoption requirements, if any, of the child's proposed residence, provided that the Attorney General is satisfied that proper care will be furnished the child if admitted to the United States, and that no biological parent or prior adoptive parent of any such child shall thereafter, by virtue of such parentage, be accorded any right, privilege, or status.

Orphan Petition—Refers to the completion and submission of a Petition to Classify Orphan as an Immediate Relative (Form I-600), in accordance with the form's instructions, along with the required supporting documents and fee, if there is not an advance processing application approved within the previous 18 months or pending, which must be signed by the married petitioner and spouse, or the unmarried petitioner.

Overseas Site—The Department of State immigrant visa-issuing post having jurisdiction over the orphan's residence, or in foreign countries in which the INS has an office or offices, with the INS office having jurisdiction over the orphan's residence.

Petitioner—A married U.S. citizen of any age, or an unmarried U.S. citizen who is at least 24 years old at the time he or she files the advance processing application and at least 25 years old at the time he or she files the orphan petition. In the case of a married couple, both of whom are U.S. citizens, either party may be the petitioner.

Prospective Adoptive Parents—A married U.S. citizen of any age and his or her spouse of any age, or an unmarried U.S. citizen who is at least 24 years old at the time he or she files the advance processing application and at least 25 years old at the time he or she files the orphan petition. The spouse of the U.S. citizen may be a citizen or an alien, however, an alien spouse must be in lawful status if residing in the United States.

Separation from Both Parents—The involuntary severance of the child from his or her parent by action of a competent authority for good cause and in accordance with the laws of the foreign-sending country. The parents must have been properly notified and granted the opportunity to contest such action. The termination of all parental rights and obligations must be permanent and unconditional.

Statute—A law.

Surviving Parent—The child's living parent when the child's other parent is dead.

Unconstitutional—Refers to a statute which conflicts with the United States Constitution rendering it void.

Ward—A person over whom a guardian is appointed to manage his or her affairs.

Witness—One who testifies to what he has seen, heard, or otherwise observed.

BIBLIOGRAPHY AND ADDITIONAL READING

Adoptive Families Magazine (Date Visited: April 2003) <http://www.adoptivefamiliesmagazine.com/>.

American Academy of Adoption Attorneys (Date Visited: April 2003) <http://www.adoptionattorneys.org/ AAAA/>.

Bureau of Citizenship and Immigration Services (BCIS) (Date Visited: April 2003) <http://www.immigration.gov/>.

Black's Law Dictionary, Fifth Edition. St. Paul, MN: West Publishing Company, 1979.

Cornell University Law School (Date Visited: April 2003) <http://www.law.cornell.edu/topics/adoption.html/>.

The Evan B. Donaldson Adoption Institute (Date Visited: April 2003) <http://www.adoptioninstitute.org/>.

International Concerns Committee for Children (Date Visited: April 2003) <http://www.iccadopt.org/>.

Joint Council on International Children's Services (JCICS) (Date Visited: April 2003) <http://www.jcics.org/>.

National Adoption Information Clearinghouse (NAIC) (Date Visited: April 2003) <http://www.calib.com/naic/>.

National Council For Adoption (Date Visited: April 2003) <http://www.ncfa-usa.org/home.html/>.

North American Council on Adoptable Children (Date Visited: April 2003) <http://www.nacac.org/>.

United States Department of Justice, Bureau of Citizenship and Immigration Services, Department of Homeland Security (Date Visited: April 2003) <http://ins.usdoj.gov/>.

United States Department of State, Bureau of Consular Affairs (Date Visited: April 2003) <http://travel.state.gov/>.

United States Department of State, International Information Programs (Date Visited: April 2003) <http://usembassy.state.gov/>.

United States Department of State, Office of Children's Issues (Date Visited: April 2003) <http://travel.state.gov/adopt.html>.